Living
WITH A
Teenager

A Survival Guide
for Parents

SUZIE HAYMAN

PIATKUS

ACKNOWLEDGEMENTS

I would like to thank Dr Fay Hutchinson, Toni Belfield and Helen Martins for their advice and help with this book, and for the continued and unfailing support they have been giving me for so long.

I would also like to thank VNC and his M24 for performing miracles in the face of fur, fangs, feathers and muddy paws, and for having shown True Character!

First published in 1988 by
Judy Piatkus (Publishers) Ltd of
5 Windmill Street, London W1P 1HF

Reissue 1994

This edition published in 1998

The moral right of the author
has been asserted

A catalogue record for this book is
available from the British Library

ISBN 0 7499 1917 5

Drawings by Jane Eccles

Phototypeset in 11/13pt Linotron Ehrhardt by
Phoenix Photosetting, Chatham
Printed and bound in Great Britain by
Mackays of Chatham PLC, Chatham, Kent

CONTENTS

INTRODUCTION

Children turn into adults. In many ways, the transitional period resembles the struggle that goes on as a caterpillar evolves into a butterfly. It can be painful to endure as a young person, but just as painful for any adult who has to wait on the sidelines and watch. As a parent, you have a hard time deciding when to help, when to intervene and when to stand back and let the emerging individual make their own mistakes and enjoy their own triumphs.

You have known them, intimately, all their lives and probably have your own ideas about who 'they' are, what they like and dislike, and what they should or should not be doing. The teenage years, adolescence, can undermine all those ideas. Your loving, beautiful and familiar caterpillar is suddenly a stranger – an argumentative, unattractive and thoroughly difficult grub. If you and your children are to survive their adolescence and even enjoy these years, you as well as they will have to adapt, change and grow. The parent-of-an-adolescent has to be a very different person to the parent-of-a-child, with different skills, new understanding and extra flexibility. You will have already found that with young children you often need to be protective and authoritarian. There are many times when their limited understanding of the world, their lesser experience – not to forget their lesser *size* – has meant you have had to guide and support them. Every parent has had to resort occasionally to the ultimatum 'Don't ask questions, just do as I say', and done so quite reasonably. But the good parent of an adolescent has to cultivate a very different style. Instead of being a director, you have to become a skilled negotiator and perfect the art, in both yourself and your teenagers, of being able to arrive at a working compromise.

For the teenager, the main task of adolescence is to learn how to cope on his or her own. If you are to succeed in *your* job, which is to encourage this, you need to foster their self-reliance, and their ability to make decisions for themselves. The firm hand must give way to the light rein and eventually you have to let go altogether.

You also have to learn to recognise when your demands, decisions and judgements are made in their best interests, and when they are made to suit you. Sometimes when dealing with teenagers, we can allow our objective good sense to become tainted with personal needs and emotional reactions. Is our son or daughter's friend really such a bad lot, or is it jealousy that makes them seem so awful? Are they really at risk in staying out late, or is it envy at the good time they are having that makes it seem so? When it comes to dealing with bolshie young teens, a healthy dose of self-awareness is as important an asset as a good sense of humour (and a full bottle of whisky!).

This book aims to be a guide for the parents of teenagers. It isn't for mothers alone, nor does it subscribe to the belief that it's only daughters that cause you heartache and worry! It's *for* both sexes and *about* both sexes.

There are several very good reasons for this. Firstly, in spite of the fact that girls and boys have certain anatomical differences, their bodies are actually remarkably similar in many respects. When it comes to puberty, most of the physical changes they experience are parallel. Secondly, whether their genitals consist of a penis or a vagina, their reactions to the fact that they are growing up are similar – fear, confusion, excitement, rebellion and much else. We tend to raise our boys and girls to have different ambitions and expectations from life in our society. We often teach them that the sexes have disparate emotional responses and needs, whereas in reality these are often the same. Boys as much as girls look for love and want to show tenderness, and girls as much as boys would like to stand up for themselves. So, when talking about puberty and adolescence, much of what has to be said applies equally to both sexes.

But more than that, the third reason is that many of the difficulties teenagers find themselves in could be lessened if they had some understanding of and sympathy for members of the other sex. We shy away from talking openly about physical development, mainly because it touches on intimate areas that many of us find difficult to discuss. This air of mystery usually results in teenagers seeing each other as alien beings on opposite sides of a secret, undeclared but very real war. In my experience as an educator and adviser to young people and their parents, rather than losing a romantic illusion about each other, a thorough grounding in the physical facts of what happens to each other's bodies during the process of growing up could be extremely beneficial. Such enlightenment and open discussion would help young people and the adults with whom they are in contact to recognise each other's strengths and difficulties and be supportive and helpful. So, even if the young members of your family are of one sex, I hope you won't feel that large parts of this book are irrelevant.

This book doesn't set out to lecture you or make you feel guilty or inadequate, or to criticise you. It can't promise the magic formula for becoming the Perfect Parent. But what I hope to do is to give you some facts and some ideas that *can* help you understand your teenagers better. Even more important, I hope to help you recognise and understand your own reactions to their needs and behaviour, and to come to a working compromise with the apparently alien beings that inhabit your home. The problem with 'How To' books and articles is that they often don't help. Real individuals and situations seldom keep to a script, so setting out '10 Foolproof Ways To Get On With Your Teenager' can soon make you feel a fool. If any of them fail, rather than blaming the idea that an outside expert can tell you how to act with your own teens, you blame yourself.

What *are* helpful are insights and strategies, not inflexible rules and instructions. By understanding what is going on, you and your teens can construct your own solutions.

In the main, parents are the best experts of their own families. But, with that statement, goes a warning. You can only be an expert at something if you have served an apprenticeship and work hard at doing well in your craft. Just holding down the job is not sufficient. Mind you, parents don't have to be perfect. What most of us aim for is to be a 'good enough' parent. Good enough to admit your love, good enough to admit your failings and good enough to come half way. The good enough compromise, after all, is not when both sides *give up* something, but when they both *gain*. The teenage years, as well as being difficult and painful, were also probably the most exciting and enjoyable in *your* life. Lucky the parents who can witness the fun their teenagers are having and regain that special glow of discovery and joy through them.

They can be perplexing, infuriating and challenging creatures as they search for their own identities and try to establish relationships among themselves and with the adults they meet. But the very contradictions they throw at you – demanding to be left to cope on their own one moment, and cuddled like babies the next – makes them all that more exhilarating. With a teenager about, dull it ain't! So, if you can remember what it was like to be a teenager and make the effort to stand in their shoes, you can help them, and yourself, survive these years. Indeed, being the parent of an adolescent can be a lot more fun and a lot less work than being the parent of a young child. If you haven't already found this true, I hope that reading this book will help you do so. When you've finished this book, you should even be able to enjoy them!

A NOTE ON LANGUAGE

At some point in the debate on how much or how soon you or other people tell your child about 'the facts of life', the knotty question about the words to be used will arise. Many parents like to think that their children, with their wide blue eyes and curly blonde hair, are innocent until corrupted by the adult world. That may be so, but calling the terms most of us use or know to be used to describe parts of the body or reproductive activities 'barrack-room language' is a fundamental mistake. Young people learn words such as 'fuck' or 'cunt', not from the barrack-room at the age of 17 or 18, but from the playground, the streets and . . . yes! . . . *their parents*, from a very early age. Trying to stop our young people using them, or pretending that they don't know them, is doomed to failure.

There are some major problems in denying that young people know and use 'dirty words'. Because they quickly learn that you disapprove or are embarrassed by these words, they learn *not* to bring them to you for explanation. They can then hear a phrase or word ('fingering', 'having a blow job', 'being careful'), find it difficult to own up to their friends that they don't know what it means, and have no-one else to ask. Many a teenage pregnancy has been started because the boy promised 'to be careful' and thought that this just meant crossing his fingers and hoping. Young people may pretend to a knowledge they don't have, and find themselves stuck in a cul-de-sac where a point of ignorance can really be dangerous.

They may also get the idea that sex is actually two things. One is Reproduction, which is explained in terms such as Intercourse, Ejaculation, Conception and possibly Masturbation. The other is what goes on by yourself or with another person, and is contained in such words as 'bonking', 'having it off' and 'wanking'. The two areas have nothing to do with each other. Which is why young people who *have* learnt all about reproduction can still get carried away and fall pregnant. They may just simply not have the words that they know *you* will accept to describe their worries and problems. To do so using their own common descriptions begs the accusation of being dirty, naughty or linguistically impoverished.

And, of course, by denying that you know or use these words, you effectively tell them that what goes on between them and their friends is part of a private teenage culture that you don't know – or don't *want* to know – anything about.

A common teenage myth is that parents don't have sex. Well, they did once (or twice or three times – once for each child!), but for parents, sex *is* only for Reproduction. It is easy to see where they get *that* idea, isn't it! When you put any barrier in the way of a young person coming to an adult for help, not asking for advice and not confiding in you soon becomes a habit.

Throughout this book, I will be using the more acceptable terms. But I think it worthwhile to go through the words and phrases your young people might use – and to remind yourself that you, in private, probably use them too! You will find a fairly comprehensive 'glossary' on pages 160–1. If you find these words degrading, debasing or exciting, you might like to consider why this is so. The best way of robbing them of any unpleasant significance or special appeal is to bring them out into the open and discuss them.

It is also worth discussing the words we use in order to recognise fully the concepts and assumptions behind them. 'Having it off' is a very different activity to 'making love'. It is significant that there are many words to describe the penis, but none specifically for the vagina, and only one, very rarely used term, for the clitoris.

It is also significant that many of the words and phrases used to describe sexual excitement and sexual intercourse are violent, hard and from the male point of view. Women, as far as popular language is concerned, are passive in sex and have things done *to* them, rather than participating in a mutual act. All this can emerge when you examine rather than ignore these words, and are important attitudes to discuss with your young people. Words in themselves have no power – only the meanings we give them. As you have probably found, whether you like it or not, there are times when discussing our sexual desires or confusions in long Latin terms is just downright silly.

1
A NEW BODY

The physical changes
of adolescence

'I can still remember how embarrassed I was when my periods started. I swore I'd never let my daughter go through that, I'd tell her all about it before she started, but I just never seemed to get round to it. I was so upset when she came home from school one day in tears. I've tried to make it up to her but I suppose you never do, do you?'

Catherine H.

'I used to take an extra shirt to school to change into at lunch-time because I sweated so much and it seemed to me that I smelt like a cage full of monkeys. I couldn't tell my mother, I was so ashamed. So I used to say I'd spilt things over them to explain why I always seemed to have so many shirts to wash. The times she'd shout at me for being a clumsy idiot! Do you know, I have no idea if Geoff has the same worries – I've never asked him.'

Frank S.

The years between childhood and adulthood are packed with a complex series of changes. Some are physical, some are emotional, some rapid and some slow. But all can be as confusing and frightening as they can be exciting and a source of pride. To be able to help your teenagers make sense of what is happening to them and to cope with it, you need to understand exactly

7

what is going on in their bodies. You also need to come to some understanding of what might be going through their minds, and we will consider this in the next chapter. In this chapter, we will look at the physical upheaval which alters a child's body into an adult's. Many parents feel that they are well informed about the physical stages and watersheds of adolescence, and you may consider the following information unnecessary. However, reminding ourselves of even the most obvious facts can often be illuminating. I have spoken to numerous parents who considered themselves fully 'clued up' on this subject who would suddenly interrupt a revisionary discussion with the cry 'Oh, so *that's* why he's acting like that!' or '*Now* I can see why she's worried!'

We often think of puberty as a specific event – the first period in a girl, or the first wet dream or voice break in a boy. In fact, puberty is an extended process that can take several years. It usually starts in girls around their tenth or eleventh year, and in boys a year or so later. However, the range of what is 'normal' can be quite wide. So it isn't unusual for these changes to start as early as nine or ten in girls or as late as 15 or 16 in boys.

Most parents will prepare their daughters for the onset of periods and many their sons for their first wet dream. Quite a few parents, however, do allow themselves to be caught unprepared. This can cause an appalling amount of fear and distress. Blood and any other unexpected discharge, after all, is usually associated with pain, damage or disease. Since, in many cases, a first period *will* arrive with some cramps and a general feeling of not being well, a young girl is likely to fear that something is wrong. If she has touched herself or masturbated, as most young people do, she may well be overcome by guilt and the conviction that she has damaged herself, or is being punished for doing something wrong. If her period starts at school or in public, most people's reaction – of mild distaste or open disgust, or a wish to spare anyone further embarrassment by hustling the girl into a private place – will confirm her fears. If yours is not a household in which periods have happily been openly discussed for as long as the young person can remember, and her primary school does not cover the subject, her first flow of blood can be upsetting. A young boy's first ejaculation can be equally alarming, especially if he too has been taught to feel guilty about his self exploration. The strong sensation and unexpected flow of semen may cause him to fear he has broken or burst something inside himself.

Whether or not they are prepared for periods or wet dreams, they may well not be prepared for all the other changes of puberty. The greatest shock an unprepared teenager can have is to discover her or his small, slim, neat and clean body suddenly transforming itself into a fat, shambling, sweaty, hairy, smelly monster, with the most embarrassing and ugly bits sprouting out all over the place. A common feature in many cries for help from teenagers is the feeling that they are out of control. Much of this fear could begin when their bodies start surprising them. Puberty prompts most young people to become introspective – to start looking at themselves and examining both their bodies and their feelings. Many will spend hours in their bedrooms or behind locked bathroom doors, staring at themselves or into space. Some will notice things they haven't spotted before – a mark on the skin, floating specks before their eyes, a slight tremor in their hands. Instead of realising they just haven't noticed this previously, they are likely to jump to the conclusion that it is a new development and heralds incurable cancer, blindness or terminal brain disease. Hypochondriacal teens may seem funny, but their distress is very real and it can lead to genuine, illness-inducing stress. If you can accept their fears and help to put them into words, and enable your young people to realise that they are not unique or alone in reacting this way, you can be a very real help to them at this time.

Both sexes will probably experience a sudden increase in height at the onset of their pubertal development. In girls, it is often the first sign of puberty, closely followed by the budding of the breasts. In boys, the first sign is usually the show of pubic hair and then the 'growth spurt'. Teenagers can grow as much as an inch or a couple of centimetres a month – a quite astonishing increase in size.

The immediate result is that young people of both sexes can become exasperatingly clumsy. There are two main reasons for this. The first is simple mechanics. Hands and feet that four weeks ago were one distance from their body are now a tiny bit further away. The simple act of reaching for a cup of coffee or walking across a room is complicated by the brain not having caught up with that fact. Teenagers have to make constant adjustments for the new size and balance of their bodies, and it frequently isn't easy. Secondly, their awkwardness is made worse by the fact that this new body often embarrasses them. Early starters may find themselves towering over classmates. They may be driven to cultivating a permanent stoop, to stop themselves being too conspicuous. Teenage girls hunch over to

hide their breasts, or walk with arms crossed in front as a defence. Boys try to control their new gangling arms, and give their hands something to do by shoving them into pockets. Rather than standing upright in the open, they slouch against walls, trying not to trip over yet one more time.

The more you criticise their clumsiness, the more they

become convinced that everyone is looking at them, and the more they stagger from one disaster to another. Criticism does not help them to slow down and be careful and deliberate in their movements. It only convinces them that they are stupid and somehow at fault. Many never recover fully, and go into adulthood with the nagging conviction that their bodies leave a lot to be desired. If we can find a baby's awkwardness endearing, and the tumbling of puppies, kittens and foals charming, we could make the effort to find gangling teens a bit more attractive! They are not being wilfully disobedient, reckless or stupid – they really *can't* help it!

Another early sign of the onset of adolescence is a gain in weight in both sexes. This should redistribute itself very quickly as long as their diet is healthy and their lives are active. Both girls and boys find their outline will alter. Girls' hips become wider and padded with a layer of fat, and their thighs fill out. Their face often becomes fuller and the voice drops a little. Boys become heavier in the shoulders, and muscles all over the body thicken. Their voices will not deepen until puberty is well under way, and their Adam's apple grows. Around the time that their body hair has thickened, boys will go through a phase when their voices 'break'. They may find they cannot stop themselves wavering between a younger, high-pitched treble and a deeper tone, especially when they are angry, excited or nervous.

In both sexes the areola, the area around the nipples, will enlarge and darken slightly. In girls, this area will bulge out-wards and develop into distinct breasts. To their acute embarrassment, as many as one in two boys will also find their nipples pushing out and heavier breast tissue developing. This is called gynaecomastia and is a perfectly normal, passing phase. It usually recedes after a few months, although it can last for 12 to 18 months. It certainly doesn't mean that the boy is turning into a woman or has anything amiss in his development.

Girls are often particularly alarmed at the reserves of fat that accumulate. In our society, slim has become synonymous with beautiful. Even young girls can be intensely fashion-conscious and be horrified when a previously svelte body begins to fill out. Telling them it is 'puppy fat' and will soon go away is likely to be met with disbelief, anger and even contempt. To a young person whose whole lifespan is measured in less than 15 years, a period of years quite genuinely also seems like a lifetime. Even puppies are only cuddly and plump for a few months! The label is dismissive and trivialising. It doesn't adequately describe a major alteration that she might feel singles her out and makes her cumbersome and ugly at a time in her life when she longs to be acceptable. Your use of such an offhand description, rather than reassuring her, may well satisfy her that you don't really understand how she is feeling.

It might be more useful to explain to her the reason why she has a new shape. Adult women *do* have greater subcutaneous or under-skin stores of fat than children or adult men. It's a survival trait to ensure that even in times of food shortage, the female body will have put something by to be able to nourish a breast-feeding baby. It's also the reason that women have greater stamina than men. Men may have greater speed and instant strength, but when it comes to trials of endurance, such as very long foot races over 50 miles, a fit woman matched against an equally fit man will come out on top. Understanding these facts might help her in the patient wait for her body to gain the height that gives the extra padding proportion, or for the extra pubertal fat to melt away.

At the same time as their bodies gain height and weight, the young adolescent will find that the texture of their skin will change and become rougher. The fine, downy hair which covers our whole body and which can look like 'peach fuzz' in a small child, will darken and coarsen. It becomes noticeable under the arms, around the genital organs and down the inside of thighs. Legs and arms may also acquire a thatch. Both sexes can find hair on their cheeks and upper lip – often too little for boys' tastes and too much for girls! Both sexes may find hair growing on their chests, and most girls find a fine ring of long hair developing around their nipples. The amount of body hair we develop is usually related to our racial group as well as individual differences. Those with Mediterranean, Asian or Jewish ancestry will have more obvious hair growth than those with Negroid or Caucasian genes.

The presence of body hair is probably one of the few developments that provoke a different response in the sexes. We tend to associate body hair with masculinity, rather than seeing it as an aspect of most mature human bodies, both male and female. While girls will accept the growth that covers their genitals and tolerate hair under the arms, any other extension can be feared. Hair on the back or buttocks, on the legs and thighs, between the breasts and around the nipples and a fine growth on the upper lip or sides of the face is often seen as abnormal. A girl with such a natural pattern of growth may be too embarrassed to undress in front of friends, family or medical personnel, and be terrified that something is wrong with her.

Our skin is the largest organ of our bodies – a 17 square feet or 1.5 square metres sense organ which also protects and insulates us. Once puberty has started, the skin becomes far more active. Teenagers will find they sweat far more than before, especially around the genital organs, under the arms and on their feet. Sweat also acquires a distinct odour. Adolescent and adult sweat contains chemical substances called pheremones. These use the sense of smell to excite our attention. We may not consciously realise it, but attraction to a particular person often starts or is made sharper through the nose rather than through the eyes. Pheremones can arouse sexual feelings, but we may respond with alarm rather than pleasure to these. Unused to this new development, young people may become aware of other people's and of their own odour, and be repelled by it. Sweat is also an ideal growing medium for bacteria. Unless the young person gets used to having to wash more often and more thoroughly than as a small child, he or she will soon be fairly 'ripe'.

Sweating not only happens when the sun is high or the body is well exercised. The sudden flushes, excitements and embarrassments of adolescence will also bring moisture to the surface. The sebaceous glands, tiny glands under the skin which produce an oil called sebum, can also cause problems at this time. Sebum functions as a built-in moisturiser, lubricating the skin and keeping it supple and healthy. The oil is supposed to ooze up out of minute pores and spread over the surface of the body. However, during the teenage years, the production of sebum can be so vigorous that minute flakes of skin can break off inside the channels and block the pores. This leads to the greatest horror of teenage life – acne. If the blockage is under the surface, it produces a white lump, or a whitehead. If the flake of skin is forced to the surface, it will blacken on exposure to air and become a blackhead. If the pressure of sebum trying to escape continues, it will rupture the wall of the channel and become infected – a spot, or as our teens often charmingly call them, 'zits'!

Teenage acne can be physically and emotionally disfiguring. Many young people become hyper-conscious of their own zits and fail to notice that it is a common difficulty – nine out of ten teenagers suffer from this scourge The over-vigorous production of sebum that produces acne is a reaction to the hormonal changes in puberty, which is why it *is* almost an occupational hazard of being an adolescent, and why it *will* pass in time.

More boys than girls get acne, and boys tend to have a more severe reaction. It might help to point out to a suffering son that it is the *male* sex hormones that are creating this ghastly rash – it could be argued that the more zits he has, the sexier he is!

Because infection and ingrained black marks are associated with dirt, many teenagers worry that acne means they are unclean. Girls who have been teased and harassed by boys often leap at the chance to taunt one who has a faceful of spots and blackheads, and can make his life miserable. In fact, the colour of blackheads has nothing to do with dirt. It is caused by a chemical reaction. The same way as skin tans in the sun, the flake of skin blocking the pore turns a dark brown when it comes into contact with the air. Washing too often and with strong soap actually has the opposite effect to that expected. Rather than 'cleaning up' the acne, it over-stimulates the sebaceous glands to turn on their oil production.

There are no easy ways to prevent or cure acne in a teenager, unless you can send them into hibernation until they reach 20! Acne isn't *caused* by eating fatty foods, chocolate or other junk food. Neither is it encouraged by late nights or masturbation. It won't go away under a regime of cold baths and dawn runs, either. A wholesome, healthy diet, good exercise and sufficient sleep will certainly make for a fitter, healthier and possibly happier young person – who may still have teenage spots! Young people have enough misery to contend with over acne without being told they cause it or could cure it if only they tried harder. Neither is true. Bad acne can drive a young person into a depression and severely damage their self-esteem. And, of course, how you define 'bad' is entirely subjective. What appears to you to be no more than a few undetectable pimples can be enough to drive your teenager into taking up sackcloth and ashes.

The natural coarsening of the skin at this age produces other fears. Most teenage girls find fine red or silver lines appearing on their breasts, stomachs and thighs. These lines – called stria – are also known as stretch marks. We usually associate them with pregnancy or old age, and they can come as quite a shock to the young virgin! Stria do not affect the skin itself, but are the result of minute bundles of fibres under the skin breaking apart. No amount of oil, cream or massage can prevent this happening or banish the lines once they are there. The only consolation is that the lines fade to a faint silver and *are*, in fact, less visible to other people than you think. Far from being a sign of old age or weight gain, they are a common side-effect of adolescence.

As fat accumulates on hips, thighs and breasts on girls and boys' shoulders fill out, so their genital organs also grow. Girls will find the opening between their legs will change shape. As a baby or child this area, called the vulva, has been a narrow slit, clearly visible when she stands up. Now, the slit will be gradually concealed by hair and will indeed move gradually downwards as the mound above it – the mons veneris or 'hill of love' – becomes padded out. In between their legs, women have three openings. Through the front one we pass waste water or urine, and this passage is called the uretha. The middle opening is to the vagina, or sex or birth passage. The back opening – the anus – leads to the back passage or rectum down which solid waste matter passes. During puberty, the skin covering our external genitals darkens in colour and coarsens in texture as hair appears. Two folds of skin stretch from the front of the genital slit back towards the anus. During this period, these folds thicken and round out. They can hang down quite some way. These are the labia or genital lips. The inner set – the labia minora or small lips – are hairless and the skin that covers them is shiny and darker in colour than the outer lips. Labia minora are often 'frilly' or wrinkled and look very untidy indeed, especially in comparison with the neat, smooth vulva the owner would remember from her childhood. The outer lips, or labia majora (the large lips), are usually covered by a growth of hair. The outer pair can hang down lower than the inner pair, or the other way round. And, indeed, some women find one side longer or thicker than the other. In front of the urethra, the labia minora come together to form a protective hood covering the most sensitive part of a woman's body – the clitoris. This too will have developed during puberty, although it has been present and sensitive from before the child's birth.

The two aspects we mostly concentrate on as being the signs of puberty – periods in girls and wet dreams in a boy – actually start some one or two years after the real event has got under way. It has been suggested that girls will not begin menstruating until their bodies have a certain proportion of fat to weight. When the time is right, the pituitary gland at the base of the brain starts sending chemical messages – called hormones – into the bloodstream, and internal organs grow as well as external ones. The uterus, or womb, doubles in size to become a pear-shaped and sized organ, situated in the pelvic cavity. The best way to visualise its position is to clench your fist, and place it against your lower stomach below the navel. If you could move 4–6 inches (10–15cm) back into your body, you'd be holding your uterus. The ovaries which are suspended on either side of the uterus also begin to work. The ovaries are two plum-shaped and sized glands, situated in the girl's pelvic cavity on either side of her uterus. Each ovary contains as many as 100,000 microscopic egg cells. Given the proper stimulus, each could grow into an egg or ovum. Each of these, given the optimum conditions, could be fertilised and grow into a baby. In practice, only 400 or so ova are released in any one woman's lifetime.

On the signal from the pituitary every month, ten to 20 ova will start to mature. As well as bringing eggs up to readiness, the ovaries send out their own chemical messages to the uterus. In response, the endometrium or lining of the uterus, starts to thicken and grow, ready for a fertilised egg. The body starts making preparations to increase the chances of sex taking place and conception occurring. The discharge or lubrication present in the vagina becomes more copious, to make sex easier and more pleasant. This liquid will have a musky odour that may not be noticeable on a conscious level but which may affect males in close contact with the woman. This lubrication is also thinner and more slippery in texture than usual, to encourage sperm to swim up through the cervix, the opening to the womb, and on to a rendezvous with an ovum.

When one of the ova is ready, it will burst out of its ovary and start the journey down the fallopian tubes towards the womb. This is called ovulation. Each ovary usually takes it in turns to release an egg, every other month, but this is by no means a rigid pattern. If sperm is encountered on the way, during a journey that can take up to a week, fertilisation may occur. A fertilised egg will complete the journey to the womb and attempt to implant itself and establish a pregnancy. Needless to say, this happens only once or a few times in a lifetime and maybe not at all. If you yourself do not frustrate this purpose, the body itself occasionally does, and even in the healthiest women more fertilised eggs are spontaneously discarded than are allowed to develop. Most of the eggs continue down, unfertilised. About 14 days after ovulation, if a fertilised egg has not implanted properly in the endometrium, the lining will come away as blood, water and a very few clots of tissue. This flow of blood is a menstrual period.

In most girls, the first months or even years of periods are 'anovular' – they occur without an egg maturing to the point of bursting out of an ovary. The signal that a first period is about to begin is often the appearance of a white or creamy discharge on the young girl's pants. This can happen for a few months before a show of blood. Some girls get warning cramps or feel tired and aching – again, sometimes for a few 'false alarms' before the first period. The actual flow can be a bright red colour, but it is just as likely to be brown or black. It can be thin and watery, or thick and full of clots. Periods can be irregular for as long as two years before they settle down to arriving in a fairly routine manner, usually every 26 to 30 days. In most cases, they last for four to five days, and the girl will lose around a half-cupful of blood each month, although it always seems more.

In boys, the development that gives them the ability to contribute to a pregnancy starts a few years later. The signal to begin the changes of puberty, as in girls, comes from the pituitary gland at the base of the brain. In boys, these hormones act on the testes – the two glands suspended below the penis, outside the body. After pubic hair has begun to grow, the male sex organs to enlarge, height and weight to increase and the muscles to become heavier, the testicles will begin to manufacture sperm – the male cells. Unlike ova in girls, these are not present in a finite number from birth but made anew each day, and as many as 300 million may be present in each ejaculation. The advantages of such conspicuous waste is that even the loss of one testicle will not affect a man's ability to start a pregnancy (and indeed if a woman loses an ovary, the other will take over!). Another advantage is that there is safety in numbers – only one sperm gets the prize and fertilises an egg, but the others aid it on its way.

A tube connects each testicle to two small glands called seminal vesicles, connected in their turn to the prostate gland. Sperm is passed up these tubes into the seminal vesicles where it combines with seminal fluid from the prostate. The resulting mixture, which is about 98 per cent fluid and 2 per cent sperm, is called semen. Semen can remain in the seminal vesicles and eventually be absorbed back into the body, as new, fresh sperm mature and travel up from the testicles. More often, it is passed out of the body as an ejaculation during masturbation or an erotic or wet dream.

Boys have erections from the time they are born. Both sexes soon learn that touching their genitals is pleasant, and even before boys' bodies manufacture semen to produce an ejaculation, or girls start menstruating, we have evidence to show that both can experience orgasm. But with the onset of sperm production, self-pleasuring does acquire an extra dimension for the young man! How often a boy has wet dreams or masturbates depends entirely on individual factors. However, it is neither abnormal nor unusual for a teenager in the throes of adolescence to have frequent emissions – as many as several a day. Boys are also constantly bedevilled by involuntary erections. An erection is the *first* response to sexual excitement. The body often reacts to a trigger – the sight, scent, sound or thought of something stimulating – even before the mind recognises it, and certainly before the penis is touched or manipulated. Adolescent boys can find themselves becoming excited in the most public places and at the most inappropriate times, without meaning or trying to become so.

Another area of confusion arises from the fact that human bodies are very rarely entirely symmetrical. Young people of both sexes are likely to find various bits growing out of proportion to others. Most of us have an arm or a leg longer than the other, and a hand or foot bigger than its twin. Boys will find one testicle hangs down lower than the other, and girls that one breast often outstrips its companion. It's common for a woman who has completed her development to find one breast is as much as a cup size larger than the other. In developing girls, this lop-sidedness is all the more likely.

Breasts are a particular source of pain and pride for young women. These secondary sexual characteristics are on show in our society, perhaps more than at any time in recorded history. When the daily newspapers with the widest circulation among young people show bared breasts every day, it's hardly surprising that both boys and girls are very breast conscious. They acquire a standard by which they judge their own or other people's breasts, without realising it is a very inaccurate one. Breasts come in all shapes and sizes and textures. Some are small, firm and pear-shaped. Others are large, soft and apple-shaped. On some, the nipples point up, and on others they droop downwards. But, whatever their appearance, they are *normal* – a fact many of us do not recognise. In most pin-up pictures, various tricks are used to idealise the body. Invisible tape supports the breast; ice cubes make the nipples stand out; and the blue veins or stretch marks that often show are concealed by make-up or neatly airbrushed out of the completed photograph.

Girls are frequently convinced that they are abnormal if their nipples do not stick out constantly, and do not realise that this part of the body is designed only to react to stimulus. The nipple is made up of erectile tissue. It fills with blood, swells and stands out if triggered to do so – by direct touch, by cold, by an emotional reaction such as fright or sexual excitement, or by exertion. At other times, the nipple can lie flat or even dimple inwards. Seeing themselves apparently different, and therefore inferior, to the model in the pictures, many girls are terrified they will be rejected by a boyfriend in the future. Worse, they fear that they will be unable to be a good mother to a baby and can become quite obsessed by their 'inadequacy'.

But when it comes to embarrassment and confusion, the changes that occur in the sexual organs at this time probably account for the greatest shocks. During puberty both sexes discover, or rediscover, the delights of self-pleasuring – masturbation. They find that their sexual organs grow. During sexual excitement, a girl's clitoris, labia, breasts and nipples swell and become tender and sensitive. A boy discovers his testicles and penis undergo the same transformation. It's hardly surprising, therefore, that many connect the permanent changes and growth with the temporary increase in size during excitement, and conclude that these alterations are freakish and a result of forbidden or abnormal practices. This is especially likely if they have been warned against 'self-abuse' and told it would harm them.

Girls have particular problems in coming to terms with their altered genitals in that not only is this often a forbidden area for them, it is also a hidden one. Our fingers are such sensitive organs that feeling an object you cannot see often makes it appear larger and rougher than it really is. Few girls are supple enough to see their own genitals, or self-confident enough to use a mirror. Their fingers do the walking, and with nothing to compare themselves against, many become quite depressed and worried about what they find. A pre-pubescent girl's genitals are smooth, neat and tidy. Adult genitals, in comparison, are quite a mess – wrinkled, hairy and irregular. Unless the young woman understands this transformation *is* normal, she may well feel her new genitals are horribly unattractive and that no man would ever want to touch or see them.

Conversely, boys can suffer from the fact that they *can* compare themselves with friends. As with any part of the body, a wide range of size and shape is normal, but most boys quickly assume that big is beautiful. The lads who are last to grow may feel – or be made to feel – that their masculinity and future sexual prowess is in question. Boys' fears are fed by two important factors. Firstly, the range of penis size is greater in a flaccid or non-erect organ than it is in the erect article. The average flaccid penis is 2¾–4½ inches (7–11cm) long, erecting to between 5½–7 inches (14–18cms). Most men will find themselves to be around 4¼ inches (10.5cm) in the normal state and 6¼ inches (15.5cm) when excited. But, a smaller limp penis is likely to swell *more* than a larger one, so that a group of men with a wide range of sizes will end up roughly equal when ready for intercourse. The boy admired in the showers for his size may well make a poorer showing than his apparently smaller friends when it comes to lovemaking. Secondly, when boys do compare themselves, they always look downwards at themselves and across at their friends. A cylindrical object hanging down will always look shorter when viewed from above than from the side. This foreshortened view gives the owner a false impression of the actual size of his own body and that of his friends. If he really wants to compare realistically, he has to do so by viewing himself and the others in a mirror, side by side!

Of course, size *isn't* everything, but it would be unrealistic not to recognise that this is, always has been and probably will be, a major preoccupation of young lads . . . and of older men, too! There are very few adult men who can honestly say that they have never worried about whether their penis was adequate or not. Rather than dismissing such worries, it's probably better to help youngsters tackle them before going on to explain that penis size has less to do with sexual prowess than have love, care, understanding and knowledge. As well as size, the shape of their organs, both in a flaccid and erect state, can cause heartache. It is common for the penis to bend to one or other side, and curve up or even downwards both when limp and when erect. It is equally common for one testicle to be suspended lower than the other. The scrotum – the bag in which they are held – can feel taut or quite loose, allowing the testicles to hang down except when sexual excitement, fear or cold pulls them up against the body.

Reading the sort of literature that tends to circulate among teenage boys leads many of them to despair if their erections are not 'ramrod straight', at an angle of 45 degrees! Such literature can also give young men the mistaken belief that their bodies' reactions should be under their control, so that a penis should be able to erect on will and not without its owner's permission. Boys who find themselves becoming visibly excited at the flimsiest excuse, can often be terrified that they are growing into uncontrollable sex fiends. They may feel that everyone can see their shame and be laughing at them. They may go to great lengths to avoid certain situations or people, or to wear baggy clothing or carry objects to hide behind, to conceal what is happening to them.

If boys are obsessed by the sexual development displayed by the size of their penis and its abilities, girls are equally absorbed with their menstrual cycle. Periods, how to manage them and how to conceal them, can form a major concern in the early teenage years. Period blood is not diseased or dirty, but as natural as any other normal discharge from the body. Like blood from a wound however, it does decay and start to smell as soon as it comes into contact with the air. Girls wearing sanitary pads or towels are bound to find that they become a bit 'whiffy', however frequently they change. The fault is not in any bad hygiene on their part, but in a simple, biological reaction.

Girls may find the idea of wearing internal protection very attractive, since it does make menstruation far less obvious, but come up against a new set of problems in this. Tampons are difficult to use if the young woman feels unhappy at touching herself intimately, and if she is afraid of the thought of anything entering the private parts of her body. Many women are unsure of the size and shape of their internal organs and so fear that a tampon could harm them or become stuck or lost deep inside them. Many parents are unhappy at the thought of their girls using tampons in case it encourages a precocious sexual knowingness. They also fear that tampon use will 'break' a girl, robbing her of her virginity. Even when these fears have not been voiced, the girl may well pick them up from you, or believe that is how you feel. She may be afraid to broach the subject, even if not using a tampon means she stands out from her schoolfriends and makes her the target for unkind teasing.

Being a virgin is not just a question of having an intact hymen or maidenhead – the thin tag of membrane that partially closes off the vagina or sex passage. Virginity consists in not having had complete sexual intercourse with a member of the opposite sex. Some girls do not even have a hymen, and in many it is stretched or broken long before puberty, by normal movement and by self exploration. A tampon is far smaller than an erect penis, so is highly unlikely to be a substitute.

It is one thing for you to feel that a girl should save her first sexual initiation for a man with whom she has a permanent and loving relationship. It is another for you to insist that the first object to breach her body must be a rampant male penis, and to ask that she endures perhaps years of discomfort, embarrass-ment and teasing to support your views. If your fears are that she may harm or hurt herself in trying to insert a tampon, the best help you can offer is a pack of the smallest size (about the dimensions of a very slim little finger) and a tube of KY or any other water-soluble lubricating jelly (*not* vaseline or petroleum jelly); a mirror and a good light; and your supportive guidance in getting the angle right and relaxing while doing so. So long as tampons are changed at least three times a day, even when the flow is slight, and as long as ordinary hygiene is observed, there is no real risk of infection from using them.

Parents give their children a pretty comprehensive sex education from the day they are born. If yours is a family that has always been open about physical and emotional matters, the result is likely to be a young person who finds the changes of adolescence relatively easy to manage, and who can and will bring any problems to you or to other trusted adults. At the other end of the scale, parents who find this an area of pain, confusion and fear will teach their youngsters to be anxious and silent. There is no such thing as a parent who *doesn't* teach on this matter – the choice is only between whether your lessons are constructive or not. Most of us are probably somewhere on the line in between these two extremes, and happy to work at doing better all the time!

Sadly, secrecy and embarrassment tend to multiply and create more misery in their wake. Boys and girls left in ignorance of their own processes, and particularly of the changes happening in the other sex, can become both intrigued and angry at the apparent mystery. Boys, for instance, often take a special delight in teasing girls about their periods, and in shouting out or writing on walls the code names associated with this event – 'jam butties', 'being on the rag', 'showing the flag' (see page 160–1). Schools often make this *worse* by segregating any classes that deal with puberty in the mistaken belief that giving boys more information would encourage this behaviour, and letting the secret out of the bag would embarrass and humiliate the girls. It's only the fact that we continue to insist it *should* be a dark and terrible secret that gives this harassment its spice. Every woman menstruates for a large part of her life – that's 52 per cent of the world's population sharing a normal, healthy event. Hardly something of which to be ashamed.

The more young people understand their own bodies and the normal changes and reactions they will be experiencing at this time, the happier they will be. Since most of us have not been helped in our youth to see these matters as anything but embarrassing, it can be difficult to approach them with ease. Young people will shy off asking us questions, not because they do not have them, but because they know they are unwelcome. They need our permission to raise these subjects. And we need our own permission to accept that we don't always have to know the answer, and we certainly don't have to keep our composure, to be doing a good job. You need a grounding in the facts to realise what may be taking place in your young person and what may be worrying them. But more than that, you need the willingness to say 'I don't know the answer to that . . . let's go and find out!'

2
AN IDENTITY
OF THEIR OWN

The emotional changes of adolescence

'Arguments, arguments, all we ever seem to get now is arguments. You can't pass the time of day with them without them wanting to make a case of it. I don't know how it happens, but it seems that any suggestion or comment I make is taken the wrong way and we just end up screaming at each other. I keep asking myself what have I done wrong because they certainly weren't like this when they were younger.'

Carole A.

Very few of us expect a baby to learn how to control his or her bowels or to walk, talk or eat on their own within a few days of being born. We know that however easily we might exercise these skills, they took years to practise and perfect. Although we may occasionally give in to irritation as a toddler struggles towards proficiency, we usually smile indulgently, feel sympathy for their clumsy attempts and give as much help and encouragement as we can.

In contrast, we often give short shrift to teenagers as they stumble their way through adolescence. We seldom recognise that the physical difficulties they face are just as momentous, indeed remarkably similar, to those frustrating a small child. They too find themselves in a new body that they must explore and learn to balance and control. We find it hard enough to understand the effect on them of noticeable physical changes. How much harder it is to accept that the *inner* person is also undergoing a transformation.

Physical maturation brings with it the ability to perform certain physical actions – to control one's hands and eyes, and to do finer and more intricate work, to run faster, jump higher and lift heavier objects than one could do as a child. And, of course, to make someone, or to become, pregnant. As the mind develops, the young person also becomes able to perform intellectual feats previously beyond their grasp.

Just as a young baby is unable to control its bowels until the musculature develops at about 15 months, so young people find it difficult to cope with certain types of thinking until their teenage years. Young children learn to deal with specific problems – solving the 'here-and-now'. They are less good at making an immediate solution a blueprint for future action. It is during adolescence that young people start to think in the abstract – to wonder 'what if . . .', and to use their imaginations to set up various situations and think their way out of them. Rather than accepting your rules and explanations, they now become more adept at constructing their own solutions. And, of course, they become more and more keen to exercise and perfect this new skill to solve any and every problem by themselves, and in their own way.

Small babies actually see themselves and their mothers as one being, and one of the revelations of early childhood is that the self is separate and different. During childhood, toddlers and youngsters, while asserting a certain amount of individuality, still regard themselves as belonging to and being part of you and the family. They define themselves primarily in relation to their parents. You, too, will feel this tie and probably never question the fact that central to your relationship with your child is the simple thought 'That person is *mine* – part of me. My job is to love, protect and nourish this being.'

In adolescence, a major change takes place in how the young person sees him or herself and in how he or she wants to be defined. Parental approval is the foundation of a child's life. One way they seek to win this is to be as much like you as possible. With adolescence, however, the answer to the question 'Who am I?' suddenly becomes less easy to answer. 'My parents' child' is no longer enough. The teenager wants to become *themself* – a person who can organise, rule and please themself. The whole of adolescence is the search for this new, embryonic adult, and the trauma of adolescence lies in how you and your teenager, separately and together, come to terms with their pulling away from your influence and control.

In the search for an adult identity, teenagers usually look outside the family for both people to copy and people to approve of them. The opinions of their own age group and of other adults with whom they have contact slowly become as, or more, important than yours. Indeed, they may well go through a stage of trying to be as *unlike* you as possible. In accepting and understanding this, do not underestimate the effect and extent of your influence. However weak it may seem during this period, it still is and will continue to be enormous.

Adults often despair of teenagers' radical beliefs and behaviour, and condemn outside influences for having led their youngsters astray. You can be tempted to exercise a degree of censorship and control over the things they see, say and do, to stop this happening. In my experience, even the most sheltered youngster will rebel and experiment, and even the most outrageous will eventually adopt a code remarkably similar to that of their parents. If you respect your own beliefs and have confidence in the way you have brought up your youngsters, the odds are that they will follow rather than reject your precepts.

As already mentioned, adolescents begin to spend time on their own, absorbed in their own thoughts and looking at their own bodies. The physical changes give them plenty to ponder and worry about. They also often create the mood itself. Emotions are often the result of chemical shifts in ourselves – you can induce a feeling of extreme well-being, for instance, by exercising your body to its physical limit. This encourages the release of substances called endorphins, which are naturally occurring opiates, into your system. Similarly, as the teenage body manufactures hormones to stimulate growth and adaptation to a mature shape, the hapless young people can find themselves swept with alternating feelings of elation and despair entirely unconnected to what might otherwise be happening in their lives.

The hormone system and our emotional moods have a complex inter-relationship. The type and amount of hormones circulating in our bloodstream at a particular time can dictate our feelings. For instance, many women feel particularly amorous midway between their periods, at ovulation. This is the time when two hormones, follicle stimulating hormone (FSH) and luteinising hormone (LH), have caused an egg to mature and be released from their ovary, ready for fertilisation and the beginning of a pregnancy. Some women feel at their most creative during their periods, when one hormone, progesterone, has just stopped being produced, another, oestrogen, is at its lowest level, and a third, FSH, is at its height.

Similarly, our feelings can affect the production of hormones. During a crisis or a change of routine – an argument, a pregnancy scare, a school examination or while on holiday – the chemical messengers that regulate the reproductive system can become unbalanced, and periods can be delayed or stopped. Any change in hormone production can bring with it unexpected emotional effects. Illness in both sexes, or pregnancy or childbirth in women, can lead to feelings of optimism and happiness, or doom and despondency. Adolescence is not an illness, but it is a kind of birth. Whatever their sex, your teenager is likely to find his or her moods fluctuating wildly as the body lurches on its journey from boy or girl to man or woman.

Just as a raging toothache would make you focus your attention on your teeth, so these waves of feeling further encourage the young person to become absorbed in themself. A concentration on the self can have various unfortunate effects. The teenager may begin to see little oddities they haven't noticed previously and become convinced that something is wrong, or that they are unusual or deformed. Their emotional instability can also be frightening to them. Some teenagers respond by becoming convinced that they are going mad. More, however, look for a concrete reason for their moods. If they are 'down', they assume that it must be because their bodies are freakish, their friends insincere or their parents unkind. If they are 'up', it must be because they are in love or about to solve the mysteries of the universe.

Unfocused grief, anger or happiness are hard to accept, so it is natural for us to look for an event or a situation to which to tie them. The unfortunate result is that the teenager often drives a bad mood further than it might otherwise have gone. He or she becomes trapped in a downward spiral, convinced that they have a good reason to go on being unhappy.

The extremes of emotional response they feel can also lead to a real phobia about being in public or in a social situation. Young people often respond to the physical changes in their bodies by becoming self-conscious and awkward. When under pressure, the body manufactures the hormone adrenalin, to hype up reactions and make us ready for fight or flight. We can flush a deep red or become pale as the blood that carries the hormone is shunted from our skin to our internal organs to prepare us to cope with an emergency. An enormous amount of energy is released, giving us that sudden, lurching feeling of having been kicked in the stomach, and we find ourselves trembling and feeling sick. Such a reaction is understandable if you stepped in front of a car or a building started to collapse on you. You would use that released energy to move yourself out of the way. With most of us, especially with teenagers in their heightened state of physical and emotional turmoil, the trigger to start a rush of adrenalin can be as simple as the sight of someone we like, or the realisation that people may be looking at us. The situation can become a vicious circle – the young person may become convinced other people can see and are laughing at their blushes, and anticipation of being laughed at is enough to trigger off another 'attack'.

Most teenagers feel shy at some time or other and suffer these normal physiological responses to fear and excitement – blushing, sweating and stammering. Those with poor self-esteem and a lack of self-confidence, however, may not realise that such a reaction is common, and could find it difficult to cope. They do need reassurance, not only that everyone feels as they do, but that many of these reactions have less to do with their *minds* – over which they may feel they should have some control – than with their bodies.

However, it would be unwise to dismiss all teenage moodiness as purely hormonal. Young people in our society have good reason to feel angry, confused and pressured at this time. Frequently it is a justified reaction to the conflicting demands put upon them. On the one hand, their bodies and minds indicate a change has occurred in themselves and in their capabilities. On the other hand, we make very little allowance and show very little recognition of this fact. 'Primitive' societies take the outward signs of puberty as a signal that the young person is ready to move from one group to another – from child to trainee adult. Once sexual characteristics appear, development in the male organs and menstruation in the woman, the adolescent is given greater responsibility and status. This is often celebrated formally in an actual ceremony, a 'rite of passage'.

Our own western rites of passage tend to come much later, on occasions such as eighteenth or twenty-first birthdays or on the announcement of engagement or a wedding. We still tend to refer to young people as 'children' or 'kids' well beyond an age at which they are physically endowed with many adult characteristics, and are legally held to be responsible for their own behaviour. Our school system, our economic system and indeed our legal system maintain, however inconsistently, the principle that young people of 16, 17, 18 or even into their twenties, are as dependent on their parents and incapable of being responsible for themselves as is an infant. At the same time, we make demands on them and put them under considerable stress by insisting that their success – or lack of it – at this time will set the pace for the rest of their lives.

When a society does not recognise the change in young people's aspirations when they become adolescents, and does not give them a framework in which to explore and experiment with their growing abilities, they will attempt to do this themselves. Adolescents constantly test themselves against the family, against other adults and against their peers to try and construct a picture of who they are and where they fit. This is likely to produce what appears to be an intense selfishness.

Teenagers are very prone to accusing everyone around them of not understanding, of not listening or of interfering or being critical – while themselves doing all these things in excess. A child who has been thoughtful and generous may, almost overnight, become literally wrapped up in his or her own thoughts and feelings, and be indifferent to anyone else's. They can emerge for brief flying visits in which they show grateful, loving concern before vanishing again to their rooms and their own preoccupations. These temporary returns to their 'old selves' can make you even more frustrated and angry with the new person, and further convinced that they are being wilful, wicked and spiteful in their behaviour.

All this introspection can lead to one of two results. Either the teenager decides that they are normal and acceptable and that things are going as they should. Or, they become convinced that they *are* different and unacceptable in some way. Lack of self-confidence and self-esteem can often slide into self-denigration and on to self-hatred. 'Agony' letters I have received from this age group often contain forceful expressions of disgust at their own bodies and apologies 'for being revolting' as they describe a perfectly normal and far from revolting thought, act or part of the body.

Teenagers need your permission to be able to ask questions and to talk about what is going on inside and outside themselves. There will be times when you will need to take the initiative in introducing certain subjects, either in conversation or by drawing their attention to a book, film or programme on the television. However, dealing with young people at this time in their lives often brings you into conflict between the need for privacy – theirs and yours – and the need for openness. Adolescence is the time when both of you walk the fine line between giving them reasonable respect and space to allow them to come to terms with themselves, and offering the right amount of direction and information to help them to do this. Privacy need not be the same as secrecy, and being open need not be the same as prying. You both may spend five years working out a mutually agreeable definition of which is which!

Parents are frequently used to having open access to their youngsters' lives. We assume that we can walk into their rooms or a bathroom when they are there, and expect them to share their thoughts with and explain their actions to us. We might feel uneasy at being excluded. What could they be up to behind that closed door? And what could they be planning or thinking behind that closed face? Their own embarrassment and confusion can result in 'silly' behaviour that can be very off-putting. Teenagers, particularly with friends, can be offhand or even crude, and fend off questions or the offer of discussion or explanations with laughter or contempt. Many parents explain their failure to discuss physical or emotional matters with their teens with the excuse 'But I can't talk to them about it – they know more than I do already!' or 'They just laugh at me!' We all hide our ignorance at times and pretend to an understanding we don't have. Young people, eager to be accepted as grown up, are all the more prone to bluff – especially when the subject is one that embarrasses them and of which they think everyone should have instinctive knowledge, such as sex.

One way of examining difficult areas without the need to confront another person face to face, is to use the written word. Teenagers, more than any other age group, keep diaries and find great comfort and excitement in noting in minute detail their thoughts and activities, their worries and hopes. Sometimes, the line between fact and fantasy can become blurred, and the events noted are more to do with wishful thinking than fact. More often however, Dear Diary is the only confidant to be trusted with the truth and whole truth of how the teenager thinks and feels. Young people are also prone to use letters, to close or distant friends or a professional adviser such as an agony aunt, to set down and clarify their confusions. These are private, as are

letters addressed to them. A parent who looks uninvited into such papers is not displaying love and care, but a prurient curiosity and a shameful desire to meddle. However, there are occasions when an invitation to peep is clearly extended. A young person may find it difficult to raise a particular subject, and deliberately lay a trail for you to pick up and comment upon.

Knowing how to start a discussion on any subject, let alone a private matter which worries or bothers you, is a skill that we all need to learn. Adolescents may drop a casual remark or query, or leave a letter or book open for you to see, in the hope that it may give you the impetus to pursue a particular topic. You need to be alert for such offhand enquiries, and it is important that your responses be immediate. Be prepared to drop everything – cooking the dinner, repairing the car, getting ready to go out –

because, once rebuffed, the young person may not be able to summon up their courage to come back to you again.

As they experiment with ways of communicating with you, your teenagers will also be learning how to get on with their peers. You may well find the degree of allegiance they give to their friends, and the importance they place on their opinions, difficult to accept. Friendships between young children can be intense, but on the whole it is during adolescence that young people find particular value in such relationships. Parents can have a certain measure of control over their childrens' contacts – they are usually chosen from families *you* find acceptable, met at school or from your own neighbourhood or own circle of friends. If a young child starts to play with someone you dislike or of whom you disapprove, you usually have the control and influence to divert them to other companionships. As your child becomes a teenager, however, you may find your power in this sphere slipping. An adolescent may want to choose friends they are fully aware you could dislike, as a way of challenging your control and as a way of demonstrating their growing ability to make their own choices.

It may not be as obvious a challenge as that, however, What is a friend? This, after all, is one of the questions young people will be exploring. A child's friend may just be someone who is at the same physical or mental level as them to share and enjoy their games. A teenager's friend may be a person with whom to explore the more important questions of loyalty, generosity, sympathy and understanding. A friend is someone who mirrors back to you who *you* are – something parents may well not be able to do at this stage since you all disagree on what this is. As adults, we have a set of rules and standards at which we have arrived after many years, with which we are comfortable. Your teenagers no longer wish to accept this package without close examination, and it is their friends who can help them unravel it all and poke around in the tangle. This doesn't mean that they are not going to come to roughly the same conclusions as you – they are most likely to do so. But, they are more likely to accept your morals and views if they can work them out themselves, rather than having them forcibly imposed upon them.

They do this by trying out new identities, by experimenting with ways of behaving, ways of dressing and ways of relating to other people. Girls, who are often brought up to be far more comfortable about emotions and far better at expressing them, tend to have special friendships in a small group or with one other girl. Boys, less easy about sharing intense feeling, tend to move in larger groups or have friendships with a specific pastime as the common bond. Girls can be personal in their discussions, disclosing their own feelings and insecurities. Boys tend to keep most of their talk general and are more likely to exaggerate their exploits than to reveal doubts. All, however, will be looking for a degree of certainty and confirmation of their own views. Because friendships are so important, not only can they be startlingly deep, they can also be frighteningly short-lived if the other person breaks the rules and shows themself to be less loyal, generous or responsive than your teenager demands.

The arguments, sudden enthusiasms and equally sudden dislikes are all a way of practising how to judge, how to choose and how to get along with other people. Your help here can be invaluable. They need to understand that these skills of befriending and talking to other people do not come naturally, but have to be acquired and practised. Most teenagers go through periods of wanting to be alone and of finding it difficult to get on with other people, both of their own age or older. Sometimes, this is from choice. Rather than insisting that they go out and make friends, or nagging at them for being lazy, respect their decision and let it run its course. But in other cases, this is because the young person is setting unreasonably high standards for what they want from a friendship, or because they are finding it difficult to make the first steps. This may come to a head when friendships with the opposite sex become important. The ability to set up a dialogue with a member of the other sex is actually no different to the ability to talk to your own. The only difference lies in your seeing the other person as somehow apart, and the relationship between you of unique and special significance.

Many young people do not see a companion of the opposite sex as a 'friend', but as 'a boyfriend' or 'a girlfriend' – a distinctly separate category. Friends are people you like, with whom you share your thoughts, time and loyalty. Boyfriends or girlfriends often remain total strangers, make each other feel acutely awkward or miserable, but stay together because possession of a partner is seen as an essential status symbol. I have received letters from teenagers as young as 12, 13, or 14, who are desperate to 'get' a boyfriend or girlfriend, thinking that their lone state makes them unusual or abnormal. Many set out, like determined hunters, to track down their prey, not realising that this single-minded approach makes them extremely uncomfortable companions.

Feeling that you have to own or be owned by a member of the opposite sex to demonstrate your attractiveness and likeability is one of the commonest and most miserable of teenage convictions. Your son or daughter will find making friends of both sexes far easier if you have helped them acquire a more relaxed attitude and the basic skills of getting on. If they are having difficulties, one way to work around them is to discuss situations you do, or have, found difficult and play-act how you would like to resolve them. We call this process 'role-play', and imagining yourself in another person's shoes or in being in control of a situation that normally defeats you, can be surprisingly helpful.

In role-play, participants agree on a basic scenario, such as 'lunchtime at school, in the corridor outside the canteen', and basic character and situation notes, such as 'John, who is 16, and wants to ask Jane, who is 15, out to a disco'. The whole family can have a go, playing the role of your teenager and the other person or persons involved in the imagined situation. This allows your teenager a chance, not only to practise how they would like to behave, but to take the other person's part to gain some insight into how they may react, and why. As a parent, it can be particularly useful to play their role and so see things from the youngster's point of view. It also allows both of you the chance to voice opinions that you might shy away from bringing up in a genuine straightforward confrontation.

Teenagers practise the skills of getting on with people in fantasy as well as in real life. While looking for friends who can reflect back to them who they *are*, they also look for 'role models' who can give them an image of who they might like to be. Media stars and athletes are chosen to be idealised figures. Initially, since it is a model for themselves that they want, most will be

attracted to members of their own sex – or figures who appear to be such. It is interesting to note that the pop singers who are deliberately marketed to appeal to younger teenage girls have a distinctly non-macho appearance!

The fantasy figure as a role model gradually gives way to the dream lover. Friendships are often training grounds for future sexual relationships in their complexity and intensity and occasionally in brief physical exploration. Both sexes may experiment with friends, touching each others' bodies or watching each other manipulate themselves. In their fantasies and dreams, young people may also find their unformed longing to be close to the object of their admiration takes on distinct sexual overtones and evolves into romantic and then frank sexual fantasy. As with all aspects of teenage development, this is common, normal and natural. Such thoughts are not perverted nor a sign of promiscuity, since they are a safe means of facing up to and exploring our feelings long before we put them into action.

Young people will be acutely sensitive about their 'crushes'. They may want to share their enthusiasm with you – showing you pictures and telling you the fascinating details of 'the loved one's' life, thoughts and ambitions. You may well find the subject tedious, the person unattractive and the whole thing either embarrassing or ludicrous. Make this clear, and you won't be telling your teenager that the two of you have *different* tastes, you will be telling them that they have *lousy* taste! Looking to other people for confirmation of their views does not mean that young people no longer *want* your approval – they do. If they don't get it, instead of changing their taste to be in line with yours, they will stop approaching you. The more you criticise, the more you object to their tastes, the more they will pull away. Life with a teenager can appear to be one unending round of carping and complaining and daily there can be new things that upset you. Part of the problem can be that as soon as you have become resigned to one craze, another replaces it. You need to be on your toes to keep up with them!

Parents do need to maintain a balance between dismissing every friendship and enthusiasm as a 'passing phase', and clinging to every utterance as if it were inscribed on tablets of stone. It is acutely embarrassing to your young person for you to ask fondly after a particular friend if the relationship was shot down in flames six weeks ago, or for you to confidently inform a neighbour that Jane wants to be a nurse if Jane gave away her nurse's outfit when she was 12 and has been into computer programming for the last year! Equally, parents can often stifle genuine interests and friendships if they refuse to take a request seriously, for instance, for a chance to spend a weekend or holiday with a particular person, or to take guitar or ski-ing lessons. The chances are that many of these passions *will* be dead ends and might involve you in wasted expense and energy. But can you place your hand on your heart and swear *you* have never been guilty of the same mistake, in the distant or recent past? And are you sure that trying and eliminating a person or a pursuit is not as necessary a lesson as finding it has value? Both are infinitely more worthwhile than never giving it a go.

Most groups will look for an outward image to express their unity between themselves and their separation from others. Among teenagers, hair styles and colours, make-up and jewellery and, of course, clothing become central to distance them from the older generation and, indeed, from other factions among their peers.

Most of us observe dress codes and conform in various ways to their conventions. We may only do this on special occasions, but whether we dress formally or casually, we would feel acutely uncomfortable or be aware of offending other people if we dressed or acted in certain times or places in an inappropriate way. Teenagers may not conform to *our* codes of dress or behaviour, but their need to conform to the codes accepted by their own group is, if anything, even stronger than ours. Parents quite reasonably complain when teenagers ask for expensive items and then only use them for a short time. We measure the life of an article of clothing in months or even years. In teenage culture, not only does fashion change more rapidly, but to wear an outdated article is to invite derision and even exclusion from the group. Keeping up with the Joneses is not a matter of status, it is often one of social survival!

Part of the difficulty parents and teenagers have at this stage is that each takes different cues from the outward show. To the teenager, even the most outrageous, provocative or aggressive style is little more than a club badge. Dyed hair, heavy make-up, extraordinary jewellery and tight, revealing or aggressive clothing does no more than give them an excuse to dress up, have fun and show off to their friends and the world at large. They may not be able to see, as you do, the interpretations that some adults, and indeed some other young people, may put on the display – an invitation to sexual intimacy, violence, or harassment on both counts. They may be fully aware of your reaction, and the more shocked and angry you become, the more successful the outfit. But, since teenagers often do not understand or share your worries about their appearance, they often find your response wildly amusing and totally out of proportion.

Parents often survey the apparent wreckage of their calm family life and complain that their teenagers are getting out of control. Looking at the boy next door, a niece or a friend's adolescent, you might be moved to say 'So-and-so doesn't act in this way. Why can't you be like them?' Rebellion takes many forms. If other parents' young people are quieter about their activities, it doesn't mean they are no less active. However obvious you may think your disagreements appear, from the outside they may be invisible. So all those other parents could be saying the same about your little angel! Take it from me, whatever goes on between you, your teenager is *not* uniquely bad, and you are not uniquely inadequate.

It can often be helpful for both adults and adolescents, for us to cast our minds back to our own adolescence and to recall our feelings and activities. If you can realise that you felt the same as your teenager, and probably became involved in similar escapades, you can appreciate their behaviour. And if you can let them in on the joke, they may accept your point of view better. Both generations are prone to believing that teenagers today invented crazy hairdos, wild clothing and premarital sex. Our generation suffered the same accusation and it was as untrue then as it is now. It can be a salutary and valuable exercise to acknowledge the similarities in you and your teenagers' feelings and behaviour. A useful way of achieving this is to get out the photograph album and look, with them, at pictures of ourselves when we were their age. This may not only provide a hilarious evening's entertainment, it should also trigger some thoughtful and helpful discussions!

3
LETTING GO

Parents' reactions to their teenagers growing up

'Have you seen her friends? They're a mess! I just can't bear it, her going around with that crew. But nothing I seem to say makes any difference. She's always been interested in how she looks, so I really can't understand how she can bear to see herself in the mirror now. I've tried offering to pay for a proper hairdo and even to buy her a new outfit, but even that doesn't have any effect.'

Anne H.

So far we have looked at the phsycial and emotional changes that are likely to occur in young people during their teenage years, and how they may react to what is happening inside *them*. In this chapter, we will be looking at what *our* responses to our teenagers' development might be, and how and why we may react in certain ways. Their transformation does not happen in a vacuum. The responses of parents and of the outside world to their explorations and discoveries will have a profound effect on their feelings about themselves and on their relationships with other people. Our reactions, too, are often a result of the complex chain of events and emotions summoned up by our having to face the emerging independence of the young person. Adult and trainee adult can find themselves caught in a spiral of exchange and counter-exchange. Both may find themselves unable to call a halt to continued confrontation and its resultant unhappiness, or to understand why they are at loggerheads. If you *can* understand what is going on, and identify the flash-points, you can often take steps to resolve your differences. There are ways of turning anger and confrontation into honest communication, and I'll be offering some suggestions on how to do so in this chapter.

However confident you are as a parent and however close and loving your family has been up until now, you *are* likely to clash heads with your youngsters as they enter their teenage years. Arguments can develop and continue throughout adolescence. To your exasperation, and in spite of apparent reasoned argument, these may never seem to be resolved. Most families argue about the same things – their teenagers' appearance, manners and behaviour, timekeeping, schoolwork, tidiness, friends, music, pocket money and responsibility for household chores.

Feelings can run high about all these matters. From being a quiet, obedient, loving, tidy and diligent child, the person sharing your house may become, almost overnight, an unbearable presence. Young children may be forgetful and even sulky when reminded to pull their weight within the family – teenagers can be openly aggressive. You can no longer overawe them with your sheer size – now they may also discover that they can seriously challenge you in the battle of willpower. Teenagers have more resources than children and they can use their developing verbal and conceptual skills to argue with you in a far more sophisticated version of 'No, shan't, don't want to!' You may answer a child's 'Why should I?' with 'Because I say so.' With teenagers, you will have to present a better argument for their listening to you.

However rational you may consider your piecemeal objections to your teenager's appearance and behaviour, your responses are coloured by one thing – an emotional reaction to their demand for independence from you. Their friends, their clothes, their music and their pastimes are all designed to say 'I no longer need you. I can make my own choices and decisions.'

You may have good reason to want to guide and advise them over many aspects of their behaviour. But the level of anxiety behind the way you attempt to do this, and the heat with which you criticise or feel about them, can often be out of proportion. It is not the money, the time or the friend that really bothers you. It is that you are rapidly losing control over someone who has been part of you, and you find this painful. In effect, your teenagers are taking steps that will make you redundant, and nobody likes to lose their job. If your main image of yourself is not as Jane or John, or as a working member of the community, but as Mum or Dad, you are going to find their attempts to pull away from your influence and care particularly hurtful. Not only are you losing a child, you are losing yourself.

Young people often enter this most vibrant period of their lives, when they are gathering their thoughts and abilities to make an assault on the future, at the very time that we might feel that our own possibilities are beginning to close up. Those of us in our late thirties or in our forties or fifties may think that our working and emotional lives are settling down, and that there will be little further progress. Indeed, we may be finding younger and more aggressive colleagues snapping at our heels. At the very time that you might need reassurance, you start being undermined in the one place you would like to feel safe – at home. Not only is your control over your teenagers slipping, you may find the uncritical and guaranteed love and admiration a child offers its parents is also evaporating. In the heat of forging their new identities and of questioning everything around them, teenagers can often lay aside or forget the fact that they love you, or at least forget to remind you of this.

Their criticisms and attacks, which can seem intensely pointed, are not actually personal but a part of a wider testing of themselves and their powers, but it hurts just the same. To have this occurring at a time when you might be losing your edge at work, and may even be feeling the years eroding your physical abilities and attractiveness, can emphasise your loss of confidence. Furthermore, your teenagers might be challenging con-

ventions that you yourself find irksome but, having accepted
them all these years as a price for being a good spouse, parent or
employee, have a vested interest in defending.

We tend to pigeonhole people in our society. Parents are
expected to behave with more dignity than carefree and irre-
sponsible youth. And when your offspring become adults them-

selves, this in turn is supposed to elevate you to the next category
of Tribal Elder. The Wise Old Wrinkly is considered to be
beyond such youthful indiscretions as having fun and making
love. You may not feel at all ready to put such things behind you,
but rather than challenge the conventions that demand such
categorising, you may see the best way of holding back the onset
of *your* 'old age' is to keep your youngsters from claiming *their*
maturity.

It can be very easy for us to feel a certain amount of envy and
jealousy towards our offspring. Not only are they starting out in
life, full of enthusiasm and apparent good health, but they do
seem to have so much more in material things than we did at
their age. This is inevitable. Goods that cost the earth when we
were young, such as hi-fi's and bicycles, are now mass produced
and cheap, and items that we had not even dreamt about, such as

personal stereos and computers, are now commonplace. However, where they may have gained in their possessions, they are less fortunate than us in other aspects. In grumbling, we ignore the pressure the availability of such plenty can put on young people, and forget the intangibles we had that they might have lost – a reasonable assurance of a job and a future in a peaceful, unpolluted world.

Young people have *always* fought with their parents. The description of their 'being prone to argument for argument's sake' is as true today as it was when first written down – by Aristotle, some 300 years before Christ! Adults have always treated the younger generation with a mixture of fondness and resentment, but the excuses for such treatment are so much greater today.

The pace of modern society means that our sons and daughters want so much more, and have access to so much more, than we did. In our annoyance at their seemingly cease-less 'Gimme, Gimme', we can forget that we, too, made exactly comparable demands on *our* parents. The teens of today want to spray their hair with gel or colour, to wear clothing we find extraordinary and to own personal steros and televisions. *We* wanted to back-comb our hair and wear mini-skirts; we now take washing machines and cars for granted, but these are consumer durables that many of our parents saw as luxuries rather than routine necessities. The *only* things that have changed from the days when we were teenagers are the objects and the styles over which we fight. The fight itself occurred between us and our parents as much and at the same level as it does between you and your teenagers. It is worth casting your mind back and trying to recall, not only what you did and how you looked, but how you disagreed with them and what you felt about such disagreements.

Many parents do not take the opportunity to examine the way they and their teenagers communicate. It seems to be one long fruitless argument, caused by their pigheadedness and laziness. *They* seem to be the ones originating all the disagreements – but

how much does *your* behaviour and attitude give them cause for
their actions? How often do you tell your teens you dislike their
hair, hate their clothes, can't stand their friends and are driven
up the wall by their music? How often do you say you can't trust
them, find them annoying, think them disloyal and ungrateful
and feel they are in your way? How much do you tease them, be
sarcastic with them, laugh at them and joke or sneer about them
and their enthusiasms? In contrast, when did you last congra-
tulate them on a job well done, admire their appearance and
abilities, say you trusted them, liked them and enjoyed their
company? Can you remember the last occasion when you asked
them for their advice or opinion, or *listened* – truly listened – to
the things they have to say? In the storms of dealing with a
growing teenager, many parents find they can get into the habit
of criticising and out of the habit of praising. And, of course, the
more you criticise, the more your teens will expect nothing
better from you, and give you further reason for hostility.

You will not be the only ones pouring on the disapproval.
Teachers, neighbours, relatives, professionals and anyone else
who comes into contact with your teenagers may well give them
a hard time. The media constantly shows adolescents in a bad
light, highlighting the conflicts and problems they can become
involved in but very rarely pointing out that the majority of
young people are *not* hooligans, vandals, drug addicts and pregnant mothers. Unfortunately, many of us take our family
disputes, add to them the media prejudices, and treat any
teenager we encounter as guilty until proved otherwise (and very
often ignore the proof, at that!). You therefore close the circle,
sending these teenagers back to their homes with even more
reason to believe all adults are against them and that there is no
point in trying to win our approval.

Teenagers, however, often *do* find adults with whom they can
communicate. You may well find young people you encounter –
nephews and nieces, neighbours or even friends of your own
children – whom you can like and understand. They may come to
you for advice or just for the occasional chat. Most teenagers

have such 'chosen adults'. They can be relatives – grandparents, aunts, uncles or much older siblings – or professionals – teachers, youth leaders – or neighbours or the relatives of their friends.

Grandparents can often be a source of great comfort. They are close enough to have a strong affection, yet a generation removed so as not to feel threatened or compromised by the new demands of the emerging adult. Grandparents can thus enjoy and approve of the experiments their grandchildren are dabbling in, and remember that their own activities were equally daring. Their youthful escapades are far enough behind them for grandparents usually to have lost any feelings of guilt or unease at the memory, while for many parents they are still close enough to be a source of embarrassment.

Both adult and young person often make an unfavourable comparison between their chosen adult or young person and their own parent or child, and wish one resembled the other. Parents who find their children going elsewhere for such help or companionship often feel angry and hurt at the implication that they have failed to provide this themselves. That your offspring seeks out other adults is far from being a sign of inadequacy in you. They need other people because it is often easier to talk about personal matters with those who are not directly involved. They also need to bounce their ideas off minds other than yours, to see if your views are confirmed or not. Having unburdened themselves, they can walk away from another adult. Sharing with you means that they have to face the possible embarrassment of having a confession of ignorance or an appeal for advice recalled the next day and held against them. The 'chosen adult' is no better than you, just as any teenager *you* find acceptable is highly unlikely to be actually better behaved or less argumentative than your offspring. The difference is that with a chosen adult, there is no pre-history, and no overwhelming need to demonstrate maturity and independence, for it is not questioned.

When talking to young people, the tone you use can not only

sabotage any chance for an immediate, constructive exchange, but set the scene for further disagreements within the family. Most of us use sarcasm and teasing at some time to get a point across. Between peers, it can be a harmless way of showing mild disapproval, or of getting a message through without being too blunt. Yet, even between people of the same age group, if *can* be a devastating weapon, used by one person in a stronger position to crush another weaker than they. When employed by an adult to a young person, it is almost always more painful than the adult realises and often intends. Younger members of the family who see its use may feel that you are encouraging them to be equally cruel, and gleefully take your cue to rag their older brothers and sisters unmercifully.

Young siblings are particularly adept at seeking out any sensitive area and attacking it. They often delight in their elders' discomfiture as they make sly or raucous comments, carry tales or let slip secrets. An angry retort from the teenager is seen as out of proportion or even as bullying, since the older child is always considered to be the stronger and to have an unfair advantage. In fact, it is the younger ones who have by far the best weapons and the real advantage. When the teen turns on you, he or she may well be accused of having a poor sense of humour – 'What's the matter? Can't you take a joke?' or of being insolent – 'Don't you speak to me/your mother like that!' Exactly the same behaviour is defined in a different way when it is done by an adult from when it is done by a young person; *I'm* teasing, *you're* cheeky. As far as sarcasm is concerned, downwards is bullying and upwards is disrespectful, and virtually whatever the teenager does he or she is in the wrong.

Underlying most arguments between teens and parents are entirely reasonable demands, concerns and requests. After all, there is nothing wrong in your wanting to know when your son or daughter plans to come home, nor in their asking for extra cash for a special event or purchase. Yet, how many times have these subjects triggered off a screaming match in your home? It is not the subject itself that touches off the disagreement, but, apart from the tone in which both of you ask and respond, it is the implications of the exchange that set you both off.

Young people are extremely touchy about their new found abilities and their wish to look after themselves. You may question their activities – staying out late, mixing with a rough crowd – out of a genuine and well-founded concern for them. All they will hear is the slight to their judgement. Frequently, the reason they cannot identify the love behind your enquiries is that it is hidden by the language that your own confusion, worry and anger produces. We often ask questions in a way that we may think is justified but that in reality forces the other person onto the defensive and allows them no room for an answer.

For instance, if your teenager comes in late and your 'question' is 'And what time do you call this?', there is no reasonable answer he or she can give. This is a *closed* question – its only intention is to make your point as strongly as possible. You are not inviting discussion, you are setting up a confrontation, since your opponent will inevitably be stung to give you a retort which you will then condemn as aggressive, insolent, disrespectful or untrue.

People argue when it is more important for them to put a point across than to listen to and understand the other person's point of view. An argument happens when one or all of the participants are more interested in imposing or insisting on their side of things, than in valuing the other person's viewpoint. In contrast, when two or more people share and listen to each others' ideas, a *discussion* takes place and such communication has a far pleasanter and more constructive outcome than a shouting match.

When your teenager does something of which you disapprove or which worries you, you have every right to make your feelings clear. But surely it would make sense to do so in a way that has a constructive result, rather than just another dispute? Rather than a *closed* question, why not try to open up yourself, the situation and them? You can make your feelings clear without stopping your offspring dead in their tracks. For instance, 'I've been very worried about you. I know you can look after yourself, but you never know who is on the streets these days. Next time you are going to be late, please let me know?' or 'I've been expecting you. You didn't say you were going to be late, so I made dinner and I'm upset it was wasted. Next time, please tell me your plans?'

In both these scenarios, you would have let the young person know *why* you felt angry, let-down or anxious, and explained why you might be standing by the door waiting to jump down their throat. You would also give them leeway to explain whether they had a good reason for irritating you. You ask them to put themselves in your shoes, and open up the way for them to explain their needs to you – such as not to look silly in front of their friends, or to miss out on a group activity. Both of you thus have a chance to adjust and come to an agreement so that in future you know what each other is feeling and wanting to do. You are not showing weakness by admitting to fear, anger or concern. Parents often want to put up a front before their children and be seen as perfect. However, your human lack of perfection will have been detected already by your super critical teenager, and the best way to win back that halo is to appeal to their sense of natural justice by facing up to your 'imperfections'.

It helps if you can examine your own rules and demands and make up your mind which of them is truly important. It's really a question of scale. If you make the same fuss over whether your daughter picks up her clothes and whether she walks home in the dark across the common, you may find she ignores a sensible warning because it just sounds like the same old nagging. If the only time you come down hard is when, for instance, you ask them *not* to get in a car with a driver who is the worse for drink, they are more likely to remember and act on what you have said.

Whether you like it or not, it is extremely difficult to impose an outside discipline on teenagers. For good reasons they will be testing the boundaries of your rules. The strength of a civilised society is that people behave well, not because otherwise they would be detected and punished, but because decent behaviour is pleasanter, more attractive and more acceptable. Self-discipline is always preferable to the rule of fear. In adolescence, young people gradually examine the rules their parents and their society have imposed on them, to see their sense and to choose to make them a part of their life. As the parent of an adolescent you need to recognise when compromise and negotiation would be more *effective* than orders or threats. There will come a time when you will be helping your teens towards becoming capable adults better by dealing with them as thinking and reasoning beings with a valid point of view, than by asking them to follow your precepts without question. This is where the art of negotiation comes in.

It may be time-consuming and you may even feel foolish at first, but you are far more likely to get somewhere by discussing areas of disagreement and finding a compromise, than by simply putting your foot down. To come to a mutually agreeable solution, you have to pretend that you are in a business or even political setting. In such, all parties concerned would bring their points of view and their demands to the table, and thrash out the best way of making sure everyone gets some satisfaction. They would then agree a contract, and write it down, so that both sides would be bound to keep to the agreed terms unless, on further discussion, everyone felt it necessary to change these. Negotiation and contracts work just as well in the family setting as they do in the world at large. Whether you write down the results of your discussions or not, using these skills can smooth the path of your relationship with your teenagers and theirs with other people.

One of the skills you would do well to develop is how to make it clear exactly what it is you find offensive. In criticising our teens' appearance, behaviour and friends, it is easy to be saying 'I find *you* disgusting, and a waste of time!' This is because we often label the person rather than the act. Instead of saying that we dislike what the person *does* – such as saying that Jane appears to be behaving in a lazy manner – we attach the criticism directly to the person, and say that Jane *is* lazy.

Labelling a person rather than their behaviour leaves very little room for manoeuvre, since most of us believe that it is difficult or impossible to alter our basic personality. Jane will soon believe, either that she *is* irredeemably lazy and there is no point in trying to alter this fact, or that she may as well act so in front of you, since nothing she does to the contrary will change your mind.

We also have to beware of a natural tendency to assume just because *our* taste is based on more years of experience than theirs, that it is intrinsically *better* taste and *right*. We often condemn the things they like as being trivial or unattractive. Their music sounds discordant, their clothes seem ugly and their friends uncouth. If they dared to say the same about *our* preferences, we would doubtless dismiss their judgement as being uninformed! Yet surely, whatever one's age, '*de gustibus non est disputandum*' – about taste, there can be no argument! The skill is to be able to say 'I love and value *you*, but I can't agree with this particular aspect of your choice. Can we agree to differ on the subject?'

You can often transform even the stormiest of parent/teenager relationships to one with a large degree of agreement if you can introduce these ideas or strategies. Cultivating the ability to ask open rather than closed questions, to have discussions rather than arguments, to label actions rather than people and to negotiate and role-play our way out of a disagreement, are all techniques we can introduce successfully to our families on our own.

Sometimes, however, the family has got to a stage where outside help is needed. There are a wide variety of organisations available, offering different levels of intervention from the friendly chat to full-blown family therapy. You should feel absolutely no shame in asking for their advice. It certainly does not indicate that you have been a failure in your job as a parent. Rather, it shows you have the sense to seek advice to fill in the gaps that were left from *your* earlier training or experience. Help is especially needed if you or your family hit a particular crisis or stress point. If someone dies, there is a divorce, separation or remarriage, or if your teenager becomes involved in drugs, you might find your own resources understandably stretched and discover that all the normal teenage/parent arguments become more acute. Specialised support and advice can be particularly helpful here, and it is certainly available.

Parents understandably want to protect their children from harm, both physical and emotional. You never want your child to suffer the trauma of a broken limb or a broken heart. The problem is that cushioning them from every danger is self-defeating. A child who has never skinned its knees never acquires the balance and judgement to avoid a really dangerous fall. A teenager who never suffers a disappointment in early love, may truly despair when a set-back eventually happens. Because you *cannot* protect them forever, it is those clumsy, stumbling attempts that you find so painful and irritating to watch that give them the necessary training to cope on their own. You *cannot* make your children's mistakes for them. They can take advice from you and need your support, but in order to learn, there are experiences they must have and mistakes they must make for themselves. Your role is not in shielding them or living their lives for them, but in equipping them to deal with life on their own terms.

When faced with a young person developing from child into adult, you really have two choices. You can go through this period feeling angry and resentful as their energy and enthusiasm makes your hair seem greyer, your body more wrinkled and your joints stiffer. Or, you can bask in their discoveries and enjoy their youth. You can learn *from* them as well as teach them, and find yourself revitalised by sharing their excitement. You can see this period, not as the beginning of the end of your family and your job as Mum and Dad, but as the beginning of a new life. As you launch your eagles out to fend for themselves, you can be secure in the knowledge that you have equipped them to deal with anything they might encounter. You and your partner can then enjoy again the freedom of a private relationship, and relax with the satisfaction of a job well done.

4
SEX AND SEXUALITY

*Self-awareness, romance and
sexual activity – how you may
react to their development*

'She's only 14, far too young to be even thinking about boys let
alone having a boyfriend. When did I first have an intense
feeling for a girl? Ah . . . well . . . yes, I think you have me there.
Yes, I can remember the first girl I really fell for, who made me
quite excited when I kissed her, and I was 12 at the time.'

Leonard T.

Perhaps the most difficult and contentious area for you and your
teenagers to discuss is their sexuality. While teenagers can be
experiencing difficulties in coming to terms with their burgeon-
ing sexual awareness, you may have the very real difficulty in
even accepting that such feelings do or should exist in them. Sex
may well be an area in which you do not feel entirely comfortable
or well-informed. Having produced a child and been in a
sexually active relationship for at least 13 years does not necessarily make you an expert in the subject, however much you or
society at large think it should!

Your unease at your teens' probable sexual interest, your fears
of their possible sexual adventuring, and the disagreements that
can arise over these, lie behind most of the arguments that come
up between parent and teenager, whatever the overt cause –
clothes, friends, time-keeping or manners. After all, what more
dramatic statement could a young person make to indicate that

they have moved from being a child towards being an adult than to establish a sexual relationship, or show an interest in having one? In denying that they are ready for this stage in their life, it may well be that you are saying that *you* are not ready to accept the loss of control this implies.

We often do not realise that there are two entirely separate elements at stake here. What your teenager is seeking to define and explore is their *sexuality*. What you are afraid they may become involved in at too early an age is *sexual activity*. Helping and encouraging your adolescent to become aware of and at home with their sexuality is *not* the same as condoning or accepting their having sex with another person.

Being comfortable with your own sexuality has nothing to do with being in a sexual relationship. Indeed, it could be argued that some of the people most settled in the awareness of their own sexuality are those who choose a life of celibacy. Certainly, many of us who are in such relationships are anything but confident and happy with the situation and our own feelings. Awareness of sexuality is, in effect, part and parcel of coming to terms with your whole self as a rounded, creative and happy human being. Young children are aware that their bodies can give them certain pleasurable sensations. In adolescence, physical changes demand that the young person be aware of greater potential in such pleasure, and emotional development leads them to realise that these sensations can involve other people and have far-reaching implications.

Someone who is aware of their sexuality openly acknowledges that they have sexual feelings and can enjoy them. They are not afraid of or guilty about these feelings, or the activities that might arise from them. They are in control of the expression of their desires and neither allow other people to misuse them nor themselves abuse others. They are sparing in how they share their sexual favours, doing so only with people for whom they care deeply. You might fear that recognising your teenagers have sexual feelings will be unlocking a box to allow all sorts of uncontrollable behaviour to get out. In my experience, it is the opposite. Trying to suppress young people's self-awareness in this area is what makes sex a frightening yet hypnotic subject, and one they rush to find out about in the only way they can – together, in snatched and furtive moments.

Their own bodies throw up insistent reminders of physical potential. As her labia and breasts develop, they will tingle and invite exploration. Sperm production will trigger erotic dreams, whether or not he has started to notice the opposite sex in his waking moments. Emotional and physical development do not necessarily go side by side, although both will feed upon each other. As the young person becomes aware that soon they *could* engage in sexual activity, they become aware of the emotional potential for a love relationship that is entirely different to the love they have had for parents, siblings, relatives or friends. Whether they are clearly conscious of it or not, they begin to explore the meaning and feeling of an attachment that has at its root sexual excitement, and the possibility of fulfilment.

At first, the strong attachments which we sometimes call 'crushes' or infatuations, may be quite separate from physical exploration. A young person might have an intense liking for an idealised figure, such as a media star, or an actual contact such as a teacher, and also be finding out how to manipulate their own body to bring them pleasure, but not actually associate one feeling with the other. Both, however, represent an area of experimentation as the young person practises what it feels like, both to yearn to be involved with another person on an intimate level, and how to experience the sexual pleasure they can have and that can go with such a relationship. They can take the discoveries they make in solitary masturbation and share them with their own peer group. Boys, particularly, might become almost competitive in this, masturbating in groups and vying with each other to see who can first produce an ejaculation, and then who in group sessions is the quickest to climax.

Rather than being worried that such behaviour might lead to their becoming homosexual, you should be concerned that the demand for 'instant results' is training them to become premature ejaculators! Counsellors who deal with men who have this problem often find that their early experiences in sexual satisfaction occurred under just such pressure. Since, during adolescence, one's sexuality is a matter of coming to terms with one's own physical responses and emotional reactions, it is normal for young people to be doing so with members of their own sex, on a common ground. Even in group activity, what is going on is basically self-pleasuring rather than a giving or sharing of sensations. It is only later that they begin to think of sexual actions in terms of a mutual activity.

Both boys and girls may be involved in sexual play with a close friend or companion. Girls, probably because their genitals are more hidden than boys, are far more discreet about their activities, to the extent of frequently not even admitting them to themselves or being aware of what they are doing. Rather than masturbating in company, they might display a similar impulse in sharing with each other an infatuation with a particular figure. In getting together to discuss this person, they can generate quite a high level of intense and sexual excitement.

You might find your teenagers' preoccupations extremely embarrassing. Because they are still at a very early stage of this development, they can, innocently, be quite open about intimate feelings we normally keep private. They also may not realise just how blatantly sexual is their interest. It is often very tempting for you to want to remove an area of discomfort by stopping the expressions that trigger it. Unfortunately, this usually has the effect, not of requesting the young person to be more discreet, but of making them feel dirty, guilty and unnatural in their behaviour. Instead of preserving your privacy and theirs, what develops is secrecy, and a conviction on their part that sex and emotional attachments are not something to discuss with you. If you want them to see you as the sort of parent they can confide in, this is the time not to drive them away in your efforts to spare your own blushes.

However, you do need to respect their need for privacy. They should be able to have time alone in their own rooms, or the bathroom, secure in the knowledge that neither you nor other members of the family will barge in, bang on the door or make loud remarks about what they might be doing in there. They might just be thinking or reading. Or, they may be looking at themselves, touching themselves or, indeed, even masturbating.

If you find it difficult to give them space and time for such exploration, you should ask yourself why it alarms or worries you. Masturbation is hardly a harmful or unusual activity, and self-pleasing brings many advantages with it. If they are familiar with their own body and its responses, they are far less likely to be caught by surprise at the overwhelming reaction they might have to someone else's caresses. How many young people have had full sexual intercourse because they did not recognise their own or their partner's sexual excitement, had not expected to become so aroused and were too astonished to call a halt? Conversely, how many couples have deep-seated and long-term sexual problems because the woman has never learnt how best to please herself, the man has only learnt to please himself – and that at a fast trot – and neither has learnt to communicate their needs to each other?

We suffer from many myths about masturbation in our society. Because it leaves you feeling drained and spent, some people fear that it weakens or harms you. Because in the throes of orgasm, you lose a certain measure of self control and become oblivious to outside stimuli, there is a fear that it can unbalance you. There is also a fear that someone who indulges in solitary pleasure will become addicted to such expression and become too selfish to be able to have proper relations with a partner. This is almost as silly as saying that practising your tennis game by knocking a ball against a garage door will make you unable to play with another person.

Another reservation, particularly about girls, is that it will make them 'too knowing', and will spoil them for the 'real thing' – intercourse with a man. Obviously if you feel that women should always be passive and only receive their sexual pleasure as a gift from men, this will be a stumbling block for you. Many

women are coming to feel that they should have as much say in
sexual relationships as men. They, too, should be able to take
the initiative both in choosing and refusing to make love, and
should have an equal right to expect sensual satisfaction as have
their partners. Many men agree with these views and find an
equal relationship more rewarding for them as well. A woman
who has not felt able to learn about her own responses may well
find the 'real thing' a real disappointment, while those who have
learnt how to please themselves can often pass on this
knowledge to a loving and willing partner.

As I have already mentioned, because certain physical
changes occur during sexual excitement, young people can
easily jump to the conclusion that aspects of their development
are abnormal, and caused by their exploratory activities. Many
are terrified that an outsider will be able to look at them and,
from some tell-tale signs, know what they have been doing.
Sexual excitement does have some quite astonishing effects on
the body. Most young people are quite unprepared and can be
alarmed when they first experience the series of changes we call
the Sexual Response Cycle. In spite of the fact that most teenagers now learn about reproduction in school, very few are told
how the human body feels and reacts as it goes through the act
that results in reproduction. Many adults, too, are in the dark on
this subject, and a high proportion of sexual and marital problems can be blamed on a lack of understanding of sexual
response. If you, as parents, are fully informed, you can pass on
these facts to your young people. Since the cycle of response is
the same whether you are masturbating on your own, masturbating with a partner or having full sexual intercourse, an understanding of what happens is as relevant to the young, solo
teenager as it is to the partnered adult.

Researchers have shown that the Sexual Response Cycle has
four distinct stages experienced equally by both sexes. These
phases are called Excitement, Plateau, Orgasmic and Resolution. The first response to excitement in the male is a rush of
blood to the penis, making it stiffen and stand away from the

body. The scrotal sac will tighten, and the testes will pull upwards. In some men, nipples will also fill with blood and become stiff and hard. Women at this Excitement stage will find the darkened area around their nipples enlarging, and the nipples themselves becoming sensitive and firm. The labia minora – the inner lips at either side of the vagina – will flush a darker colour, the vagina become moist and the clitoris engorge and increase in size.

Excitement can last from a few minutes to a few hours, and can be triggered and continued by thoughts or dreams as well as by touch. Contrary to popular opinion, women are no slower to excite than men. Excitement, however, can start long before actual loveplay has begun, so if it is the man who has initiated the encounter, he may well be far into the Excitement phase before his partner even has a chance to begin. If he then concentrates on his own pleasure, and she has no opportunity to show him which caresses she prefers, she may well be left stranded halfway through the cycle when he has already finished.

In the next, Plateau, phase, both sexes will find their bodies flushing a mottled pink or red, especially on the face, neck, chest, stomach, shoulders and arms. Both will find their hearts racing and their breathing becoming heavier. The male finds his penis enlarging still further, with the glans or tip flushing a deep red, while his testes may have increased in size by as much as 50 per cent. A few drops of fluid that could contain sperm will ooze out of the penis. The female finds her labia altered in size and shape, either flattening against her body or thickening and hanging down and becoming an even deeper red or purple in colour. Her breasts will increase by as much as a quarter in size. She may find her vagina moist to the point of wetness.

On Orgasm, both will spasm, as he ejaculates and she has a series of rhythmic vaginal contractions. Over the next half an hour or so, Resolution will occur, when everything will return to its resting size and colour – unless, that is, the four stages have been interrupted. A person aroused but not satisfied may find the tumescent or erect areas take as long as several hours to subside and could be sore and congested. They may feel tense and unhappy. Courting teens are particularly prone to experiencing this, as they excite each other but refrain from going 'all the way'. Boys can often be terrified that their aching scrotums are the result of their having broken something inside themselves.

As well as the opportunity to be physically alone, many teens at this time need their *emotional* privacy to be respected. You are invading their territory, not only if you continue to go into their rooms and rummage about their belongings as if you have every right to do so, but also if you demand that they account for every moment and every thought. You may feel you do have this right, and that is why you and your teenager could have some very painful head-on clashes. It is not only their sexual responses that are developing, it is a feeling of themselves as a separate being from you, and one who is entitled to his or her own opinions and life. You would feel outraged if your children opened your letters, went through your drawers or rearranged your belongings. While such behaviour is accepted from their parents by children, it is a source of real anguish in teenagers. Your argument may be that it is the only way you can look after them properly and protect them from harm. What you need to ask yourself is at what stage this level of supervision is because of true concern for their well-being, and when it is for yours.

There comes a stage when the emerging adult could take responsibility for some of their own affairs if only you let them, but to do so would mean a loss on your part. Some parents react to the possibility of this loss of control by attempting to ignore or hold back their offsprings' explorations. Many indulge in teasing, which they might excuse as being harmless or even necessary, on the grounds that youngsters need to learn to take a joke and not take themselves so seriously. Teasing and sarcasm are also easy devices to hide behind in order to avoid direct confrontation, and so as not to be accused of criticising. Since sex is an area in which most of us feel vulnerable, it is particularly easy to humiliate a young person over their developing sexuality and their newly awakening sexual feelings, and to leave them with lasting difficulties. Many rapists, for instance, have had the common experience of having been mistreated this way in their youth, making sexual arousal a source of anger and pain, rather than joy.

Whatever your reaction to their solitary activities or crushes, many attitudes will come to a head on the arrival of the first special friend of the opposite sex. You are quite likely to find yourself giving tongue to the age-old and plaintive litany, 'You're too young.' 'What about your studies?' 'She/he is awful,' and 'What will the neighbours think?' It's a worthwhile exercise to cast your mind back to your own youth and to be honest with yourself about your past feelings and behaviour. Even if you are reluctant to admit it to others, recall for yourself the first time *you* had an intense feeling for another person. Most of us have a selective amnesia about our own past – we insist that our off-spring are still children at an age when *we* had far from 'childish' feelings and, indeed, were involved in far from 'childish' activi-ties. If we had to specify an age at which we think our children should become interested in sex, it is invariably at a few years older than they are at that moment – and a few years later than *we* waited!

We can divide our objections to our young people's sexual exploration into two areas; the emotional response and the rational argument. The first often colours the second, and it is our confusion between the two that stops us explaining our-selves to our young people in a way they can understand and accept. All teenagers have sophisticated hypocrisy detectors and, even if you don't see it in yourself, will know when an objection has a personal basis. In dismissing your views as being due to jealousy, envy, selfishness or simply old age, they will miss your genuine concern and good sense. If you want them to accept the package, you do have to examine it yourself to see how and why you are saying certain things.

As I have already indicated, parents have a good reason to resist their offsprings' entry into the world of adult sexuality, since for many of us this seems to herald our own exit into the genteel stage of being a non-sexual golden oldie. All too often, parents and teenagers accept the idea that we are two different categories of human being – the 'sexually active young and beautiful' and the 'sexually neutral old and wrinkly'.

Being a parent does *not* necessarily mean that you were sexually chaste before your marriage, or that since then you have only engaged in reproductive – not *sexual* – activity. Many parents try to pretend the former, and many teenagers believe the latter! In fact, statistics suggest that almost three-quarters of couples married in the early seventies – the parents of many of today's teenagers – slept with their partners before marriage. You may find communication easier at this time if you can bring yourself to point this out. This is not to say that you should confront your young person with your own sex life or sexual desires. There is nothing prudish in respecting the barriers a natural wish for privacy erects between you on this. However, your teenagers are more likely to talk to you about their inner-most feelings if you can acknowledge that members of your generation might not have been so abstemious after all, and that Mum and Dad haven't exactly forgotten what it's all about.

When teenagers show an interest in a member of their peer group, it is not unusual or unnatural for the parent to feel betrayed and discarded. After all, until this moment you were the one your teenager loved best. The husband who has an extra-marital affair with a younger woman at this time may not really be looking for a sexual partner, but be trying to find a substitute for the uncritical love his daughter once had, but no longer seems to have, for him. Little girls practise their developing attractiveness on their fathers, learning how to charm and get on with a future partner through him. The child almost certainly resembles her mother and can recall to his mind the early days of courtship. When a boy comes on the scene, it would be difficult *not* to see him as a rival – and a spotty, unworthy one at that! Mothers can have exactly the same bond with their sons, and both parents may compare their rivals with themselves, and find them wanting.

You may be horrified to think of your son or daughter in sexual terms, and be extremely reluctant to accept their sexuality, yet find yourself very quickly imagining a sexual content in their boyfriend's or girlfriend's intentions. The other person becomes a convenient scapegoat – instead of facing up to the fact that your teenager is growing up, you can blame the intruder for any sexual activity and believe that your innocent was led or forced into it.

Young teenagers' first ventures into love are likely to be intense and all-consuming, but more romantic than sexual in nature. Left to themselves, young people will probably progress very slowly from admiring each other from afar, to exchanging first words, dating, hand holding and kissing. It may be ages before they get to the stage of even wanting to explore each others' bodies – if they ever do. Paradoxically, it can be adults' *expectations* of their relationship being sexual that can force them into taking it that far. If you work yourself into knots preventing them ever being alone, and issue dire but vague warnings on the consequences of 'letting things get out of hand', you may well provoke the very thing you are trying to prevent. After all, if they have been given the label, they may as well go ahead and enjoy the act.

Parents often leap to conclusions because behaviour and dress have changed since our day. A girl in black tights or wearing an ankle chain, a skimpy dress or having dyed hair might, to us, have been showing a certain level of sexual experience or invitation. A man with a ring in the left ear and bright coloured clothing was wearing the acknowledged badge of homosexuality. Now, all these are everyday styles with no special significance. Also, some of our youngsters have a greater degree of physical and verbal ease with each other than we had, and many of the things they say and do together which in our day would only have passed between lovers, merely indicate friendship. If your teen's friendship is tender and romantic and you coarsen it in their eyes by distrusting them, they are far less likely to come to you later if or when they do need advice in a relationship that is becoming physical. You can accept their loving feelings for each other and acknowledge their desires, without condoning or prompting sexual activity.

Our greatest fear as parents is often that young people *will* have sex too early, and that this will in some way harm them. Why *do* we object to early sex? You may think the reasons are self evident and obvious. They do, however, bear examination. Common arguments are that a too early sexual relationship:

> can lead to emotional damage.
> can lead to physical harm.
> can lead to pregnancy.
> can lead to sexually transmitted disease.
> can take their minds off education and careers.
> can lead to an unsuitable marriage.

Of course, the greatest anxiety parents acknowledge, especially those with daughters, is that an unwanted pregnancy will occur. Logically, if this were your only concern, the sensible action would be to encourage your daughters to seek contraceptive advice if and when they became involved. We are, on the whole, far from logical!

Pregnancy is not always the result of ignorance or accident. For some, it happens as the result of a conscious or unconscious weighing up of costs and benefits. The costs of a sexual relationship are arguments with you, and the risk of pregnancy. The benefits are the status of having a steady girlfriend or boyfriend, the affection he or she might offer, the feeling of adulthood and the sheer sexual pleasure. The costs of not using a method of birth control are the risk of pregnancy and all the problems that brings. But the benefits are that they avoid the enormous hassle of *getting* contraception, the arguments your finding it would produce, the reputation using it might give them, and having to admit to being sexual.

If they do get pregnant, this in itself may have some benefits such as giving them status or, for a young person who does not have a career or even a job in prospect, something to do.

Pregnancy is also a powerful weapon to be used against parents who are refusing to let them grow up, and an effective way of showing their anger at or disagreement with you.

Sex is itself often seen as an explosive force – an elemental power that can control you, damage you and possess you. It is not only its consequences that we wish to avoid. If we find our

own sexuality problematical as adults, how much more difficult, we assume, it must be for a 'child' to cope? Remembering the pangs of our own first love, we seek to protect our own from that pain. However, painful experiences are an essential part of growing up, and the more one is protected from them, the less well one is able to manage. In *any* activity, one has to serve an apprenticeship. Trying to cut this short or delay it does not produce a skilled craftsman, but one who is at risk of damaging themself and anyone around them when they *are* put in a position of responsibility. The very fact that your young person is experiencing these feelings proves that they *are* at the stage of being ready to learn to understand and cope with them. Our mistake is in assuming that the depth of emotion and commitment they may be feeling, and the significance they attach to such a relationship, means that they are having full sexual intercourse.

The argument that teenage love interrupts their studies is glib, but hardly reasonable. The fact that our educational system makes demands on them at the same time as they are experiencing their first strong attachment, is society's bad management, not their fault. Nature is no respecter of examinations, and they cannot be blamed for finding their minds are engaged in more important things than schoolwork or jobs.

We add to their load if we insist that they *shouldn't* be thinking about these matters. Instead of being able to shunt their romantic affairs aside, as we demand, the result is that they have to contend with your disapproval *as well* as their homework and their romance. Keeping feelings or even meetings a secret adds considerably to the time and effort spent on the boy or girlfriend.

Furthermore, a relationship conducted against the odds and in the face of your disapproval, acquires a certain glamour. Many a young person has persisted with a boy or girlfriend of whom they have grown tired or who even makes them miserable, rather than admit that you were right. Opposition to a relationship and an insistence that they are too young is also more likely to result in early marriage. In such a situation, marriage is seen as the only way of establishing their right to be with the loved one, and of proving their maturity. How much better for all concerned if the couple had been left without pressures to see if the friendship would develop or peter out on its own.

Which brings us back to *why* we object to the thought of our offspring having sex, and *what* we can do about it. Studies on teenage sexual experience (summarised in the Guttmacher Report of 1986) show that young people who have early sex are *less* likely to have talked to their parents or have had an easy relationship with them; are *less* likely to be well informed about sexual matters and *more* likely to have found out the facts of life from friends than from teachers or parents. We know that when young people can talk to adults and not only learn the facts but discuss their feelings, and when they have free access to counselling and birth control, the rates for pregnancies and abortion are far lower than when they are kept in the dark and in silence. If we would like to discourage our young people from early experimentation, it follows that we are more likely to be effective in this if we satisfy their normal curiosity than if we leave them to learn among themselves. We are also more likely to succeed if we don't make *all* sexual expression the enviable and exclusive preserve of adults. There is nothing quite as challenging to a young person starting to grow up than to be told 'This is not for you, because you are too young.' Hardly surprising that he or she will grasp at proving their maturity by smoking, drinking and making love, 'just like an adult'.

A lack of complete honesty between adults and young people can also lead to a curious perceived division between what *you* are warning them against, and what *they* are getting up to. Some young people know all about Reproduction and Sexual Intercourse – it's what goes on between married couples and rabbits, and its only function is to produce babies! What happens between John and Jane at 4 o'clock one afternoon while playing records in his room, or at 9 o'clock one night while babysitting, is something else entirely, has nothing to do with your warnings and is totally beyond your comprehension. As you might have made clear, Parents Don't Do That – so how *could* you understand?

So, if you want them to 'be careful', you would do better to be explicit and acknowledge that they may *want* to experience this very human, normal and most pleasant of activities. As a way of keeping them in line, threats of retribution can self-destruct. It is quite reasonable to inform them of sexually transmitted diseases and the risks of pregnancy. If, however, all you do is warn them that they are the inevitable results of sex, and they or their friends take a risk and get away with it, an entire group of young people can become convinced that *everything* you have said is so much rubbish. The bogey man approach is only effective if he *does* appear at the first transgression! If not, the young person is likely to go on ahead until disaster *does* strike.

Furthermore, condemning young sexual activity as being promiscuous, or dismissing it as being trivial, are both counter-productive. Young people do *not* see their early, premarital sexual relationships as promiscuous or casual. We tend to view any short-term relationship as being less important than a life-time commitment. To a lovelorn 15-year-old, their passion *is* for life, and nothing a cynical adult can say will convince them otherwise. First love is arguably the most intense and violent passion we will ever feel. They can quite genuinely believe that they will die or never recover if anything goes wrong. To call it 'puppy love' is to unfairly belittle a very real emotion and show a lack of understanding, sympathy and respect that does you no credit. Making little of it will not make them take themselves less seriously, but it will drive them away from confiding in you.

We don't see learning to love as a central part of a young person's development, as we do perhaps view their struggles to learn to read, write or add up. Yet, it is perhaps the most important of life's skills. Did you tease them in the same way about their first writing efforts as you might about their first date? Of course, you can reassure yourself, as long as you do so in private, that their first loves *are* unlikely to be their last. So, *his* obsession with a punk and *her* unfortunate involvement with a greasy biker do not necessarily represent irrevocable choices. But you would be unwise to express your doubts to your son or daughter. Not only would this drive them away from you, your fears could be groundless. Underneath the 'uniform', both these partners might be charming and delightful young people, and they may not be leading your adolescent astray as you believe.

Young people tend to be monogamous – faithful to one person. They are, however, more likely than adults to be involved in 'serial monogamy' – that is, not a collection of casual relationships, but a string of serious ones. These only last a relatively brief time, not because the person involved is unable to make commitments or is casual about their sexual behaviour, but because the nature of this time of life is that they are continually developing and refining their tastes, and moving on to new enthusiasms and people. If your youngsters have the chance to get to know a range of people, they are more likely, when they do settle to a life partner, to choose the right one and not just the first one. Considering the fact that we now tend to marry in our mid twenties and live until our mid seventies, it is not unreasonable to ask which you would prefer – that your offspring searches for the ideal *before* they get married . . . or after?

The grazed knees a child suffers while learning to walk are not only small and temporary hurts, but essential learning aids. Most of the heartaches and quarrels of adolescence can be seen in the same light. There are, however, a few experiences we could all do without, such as causing or having an unwanted pregnancy. There are three ways in which you can attempt to avoid such an event. You can apply rigorous control and discipline on your youngsters, putting the fear of all kinds of retribution into them, and deliberately frustrating any sort of contact with the opposite sex. You can put your daughter on the pill or issue your son with condoms. Or, you can alight anywhere on the line between these two extremes.

The first option may be appealing as it seems to be the most effective. However, apart from being very hard work, it actually has a very low success rate. As parents throughout the ages have sadly discovered, confining adolescents, whether physically or intellectually, is the perfect way to incite them to rebellion and to focus their minds on the very thing you are forbidding. It might work in an isolated or rigid society where everyone has the same views. In Western society where the media uses our sexuality to sell us goods and manipulate us, it is almost impossible to prevent your young people from obtaining some level of sexual awareness, and you *can't* keep them in ignorance.

What you can do is to arm them against misinformation, misunderstanding and misinterpretation, and you do that by *increasing* their knowledge. We often say that 'a little learning is a dangerous thing', and use this as an argument for keeping people, particularly young people, in ignorance. The author, Alexander Pope, would be horrified, as his original intention was to say exactly the opposite. It is only a *little* learning that is harmful – proper understanding is what we need and should search out:

> 'A little learning is a dangerous thing;
> Drink deep, or taste not the Pierian spring:
> There shallow draughts intoxicate the brain,
> And drinking largely sobers us again.'

This could well be a good motto for all parents! We also say that ignorance is bliss, and insist that youthful innocence is somehow blighted and sullied by knowledge. From the letters I have received, I am convinced that *nothing* blights innocence more than the mistakes young people make because they didn't have the facts at their fingertips, and felt unable to talk to either adults or their peers about their confusion.

Going to the other extreme, however, can be just as harmful. Insisting that your offspring be equipped for intercourse as soon as they reach puberty or acquire friends of the opposite sex can be forcing an issue that doesn't yet have relevance. You also insinuate yourself into a part of your teenager's life that should be separate from you. Their *sexuality* may depend heavily on your acceptance and approval, but their first *sexual encounters* need to be their own – with people *they* choose and at a time they choose. If you try to annexe this stage of their development, instead of encouraging their gradual maturation, you hold them back.

Some parents pride themselves on being their teenager's chum or friend, and see explicit discussion of their young one's sex life as being part of this. This 'openness' tends to only go one way, from teenager to parent! Certainly, you do need to have a different, less authoritarian and more equal relationship with your child-as-teenager than your child-as-child. But he or she *still* needs you to be a *parent*. Crossing the boundary to sexual confidant or participant deprives them of your support and care as an older and uninvolved presence. It also violates a very important barrier between parent and child – the 'incest taboo'.

Directing their sex lives to this extent, and getting your own satisfaction from your youngster's escapades is akin to taking part in them and this, whether you touch, look, or listen to detailed reports, is dangerous and unhealthy for all concerned.

Giving them information about contraception and how to get it, and letting them know that you would rather they were safe than sorry, is another matter. Just as with road safety drills, you would do well to impart this knowledge some time before they actually need it. People go ahead and have sex for a number of reasons – knowing about and having access to contraception *never* has been shown, in all the studies done on the subject, to have any effect on their decision. Rest assured that telling them about birth control is *not* going to make them experiment early. Instead of directing them to use a method whether they need to or not, your aim is to give them permission to come to you or another responsible adult for advice and help if they so choose, when they need it.

Warnings about the dangers of birth control and promiscuous sex appear to have a deterrent value opposite to the one you might wish. It doesn't stop them having sex, it just puts them off using precautions. Indeed, the message most young people get from their parents is that 'bad girls' are on the pill, so the best way to prove that *you* are good, pure (and just allowing yourself to be swept away with love) is *not* to use anything! Research shows that, contrary to this myth, the less established a relation-ship, the *less* likely it is that the couple will be using a method of birth control. Girls who are in the worst position to cope with an unintended pregnancy are the ones most likely to suffer one.

Many young people resist the idea of using birth control because it requires that they openly acknowledge that they are sexually active. They cling to the idea that romantic love would be ruined by 'cold' advance planning, such as is necessary if they are to obtain birth control. In being unable to accept their sexuality, they have to deny the reality of their sexual desires and activity, and the inevitable consequences. They see it as prefer-able for the girl to become a 'little bit' pregnant by being carried away, than for them to come out and freely admit that they wanted to make love.

Keeping in mind the facts shown by studies on the subject, that young people who have access to birth control do not become sexually active earlier, or have more partners or make love more often than those who cannot get contraception, you may decide that it is a good idea to discuss methods with your teenagers. Not doing so will not stop them making love. Doing so will not encourage them to make love. But if they do take this step, surely it is preferable that they do so with as little risk as possible?

Certain methods of birth control may be better suited to young people than others. The pill may be appropriate where it is particularly important that the user does not become pregnant. Someone in the throes of getting qualifications or starting a new job might find this essential. Doctors do advise that regular periods should have been established for at least two years before going on the pill, and some women do experience uncomfortable side effects from this medication. The pill could also increase some women's risks of suffering certain illnesses and difficulties. However, it is vital to note that around three million women in the UK take the pill, that it *is* the most researched drug in contemporary use, and that the number of women who are taken ill or die from its effects is vastly overshadowed by the number who are made ill or die from pregnancy – leaving aside for the moment the problems of unintended pregnancy! Rather that putting your daughter off the idea of going on the pill, it could be better to advise her to talk to a doctor about it, for him or her to assess their medical suitability.

Intrauterine Contraceptive Devices (IUCDs or coils) are no longer considered to be a good option for young people. They do have a risk of encouraging pelvic inflammation from bacteria carried into the womb via the strings attached to the device.

Barrier methods such as the cap or condoms are thought to be ideal. Not only do they protect against sexually transmitted diseases (STDs) as well as pregnancy, but they remove the extra risk a young woman has of developing cancer of the cervix if she has early intercourse. They are also a method that can be used spontaneously. Young people are notoriously prone to breaking and restoring relationships. Girls on the pill who have an argument with their boyfriend are likely to throw away their supplies – and then get pregnant at the reunion! Alternatively, they will have unprotected intercourse with a new partner for a few cycles before again seeking help. If she were using a cap, or he condoms, this risky period would not occur.

Condoms have suffered from an image problem. We tend to associate them with illicit and dirty sex, although, in fact, they are used primarily by married couples. To be honest, at the heart of most of the complaints about condoms – that they are awkward, unpleasant and reduce your pleasure – is the fact that most men are too embarrassed to use them. They are afraid that their fumblings will show a lack of expertise and that they might lose their erection or come too soon. Condoms can offer a measure of protection against HIV, the virus that causes AIDS, fears about which have prompted medical experts and the authorities to promote their use. They are rapidly becoming a fashion accessory. Filofax, some jeans and underpants even have a trendy condom pocket! It is to be hoped that in the future, just as young men now swot for their exams and practise for their driving test, they may experiment on their own the technique of putting on a condom for future reference.

Young people can approach any doctor for advice and a prescription for contraception. It is obviously preferable that they be seen by the family doctor, who has access to full knowledge of any health risks. If you and your own doctor put barriers in the way of such an approach being made, you are unlikely to prevent sex taking place, but you are increasing the possibility of its having unpleasant consequences. A doctor who does see and advise a teenager will be doing so in their best interests, and is almost certainly going to suggest that they discuss the matter with their parents.

If a teenager is over 16, they are legally able to request and be given contraception without their parents being asked for permission. In the case of an under 16-year-old, as long as the young person is felt to be of 'sufficient understanding' they too can make such a request on their own.

It is worth noting that a young person who has the support of their parents and good self-esteem, and who has chosen to have a sexual relationship, is no less able to use contraception efficiently than an adult. The belief that giving contraception to teenagers only increases their risks of getting pregnant is disproved by a large body of evidence.

It is also wrong to believe that young people are cavalier about the risks of pregnancy and see abortion as an automatic safety net. For a start, most teenagers are highly idealistic and see abortion as unacceptable. They would certainly not take account of the possibility in their planning. However, theory and practicalities are often far apart and when faced with a pregnancy or the three options – a shotgun wedding, giving birth to an illegitimate child or having an abortion – most teenagers resort to the last. An abortion is legal in this country if two doctors agree that the woman has good medical, emotional or social reasons to justify it. The doctors concerned are usually the family doctor or a doctor from a family planning or youth advisory clinic, and a hospital or abortion clinic surgeon. The operation is available on the National Health to married or unmarried women of any age. However, in some cases, women are forced or choose to go to one of the charities offering such help.

Abortion is an emotive subject and women do not have this operation lightly. However, it is untrue to say that a woman will necessarily be emotionally or physically scarred by the experience. Proper counselling from her medical advisers and sympathetic support from her friends and family will enable her to make the right decision and not to regret it. As long as the operation is done as early as possible by competent medical staff, she is actually at less risk than if she went ahead with the pregnancy.

Under the original terms of the 1967 Abortion Act, abortions were legal if two doctors agreed certain criteria have been met and the operation was done before the foetus had developed to a point where it was capable of being born alive. This was usually understood to have an upper time limit of 28 weeks, although advances in medical practice in the 1980s brought this ceiling down to as early as 23 or 24 weeks. Changes in the law in 1990 set an upper limit of 24 weeks. Since a pregnancy is calculated from the first day of the last menstrual period, and this is not always easy to recall, most doctors make their deadline far earlier.

Most National Health hospitals will not accept operations on women over 12 weeks pregnant. For this reason, anyone needing to discuss an abortion with their doctor really must see him or her as soon as the first period is missed. A doctor would always want to involve the parents of a young person still living at home but it must be remembered that, whatever her age, it is *her* pregnancy and *her* body that is involved. Even an under 16-year-old has the right to refuse or request to have an abortion, whatever their parents' views are on the matter.

Just as they will resist accepting the need for birth control, young people will often shy away from recognising that they might be at risk of STDs. These are thought to be associated only with casual sex and dirty people – and have no relevance to *their* romantic love. In talking about this with your young people, it is therefore important to be able to put aside the moral overtones that we often place on STDs. They are *not* diseases that are a punishment for wrong doing, or a result of 'bad' sex. AIDS virus does not know its carrier is gay, and gonorrhoea is unable to check whether its new victim is experienced or a virgin before taking up residence. Indeed, you can catch an STD on your wedding night as a virgin from your virgin-but-for-one-experience spouse!

There are quite a few infections of the reproductive organs that are not actually sexually transmitted – such as Thrush or Cystitis. Terrified of being accused of misbehaving, many teenagers suffer these in silence rather than go for advice to a doctor or speak to their parents.

It has been said that, with AIDS hanging over them, the next generation will have to be more responsible and less promiscuous in their sexual relationships. However, human beings respond badly and illogically to threats. Recent surveys have shown that young people are aware of the risks of AIDS. They know that it is no longer confined to a 'high-risk' group of people, but can affect anyone, and that there are certain activities to be avoided and precautions to be taken. However, hardly any of them are acting on that knowledge.

We all, and teenagers more than most, see ourselves as immortal – the unthinkable only happens to other people. Unless we can help our teenagers to see genital infections as something that *any* sexually active person can catch, and indeed in some cases develop spontaneously without having to be passed on, we do not help them. Unless we are willing to teach them the practicalities of safer sex, we do not protect them. By all means, urge them to be chaste. But also urge them to be choosey if they won't be chaste, and to take precautions. Non-penetrative loveplay – 'petting' or mutual masturbation – is safer than intercourse. If sex *is* to take place, then it should be with a barrier method, and one of the spermicidal creams or gels that contains nonoxynol-9, an ingredient that appears to destroy the AIDS virus and other STDs.

If the thought of giving such advice appalls you, consider this. That your son of daughter remains a quiet and obedient virgin until marriage may not be within your power. Your choice may be between having a healthy, live teenager who is doing something with which you disagree, or one who is sterile from a hidden, untreated infection or dying from AIDS. Which would you prefer?

It would be helpful for young people to be aware of the symptoms that might indicate a genital infection, whether sexually transmitted or not, and for them to feel able to ask a doctor for advice and help. In girls, a musky-smelling fluid that dries to a white or cream stain on the pants is more than likely to be normal vaginal lubrication. However, any vaginal discharge that is yellow or green, has a foaming or curd-like consistency and smells positively unpleasant, should be investigated. So should a discharge from the penis, or pain on passing water, itching or rashes in the genital area of either sex.

When your offspring finally do let slip the fact that they have a boy or girlfriend, how are you to react? Some parents, as we have already mentioned, do so with criticism or animosity, in an attempt to keep their young people in check. They reveal their jealousy and possessiveness by finding fault with their 'rival' and belittle them to, or in the hearing of, their teenager. Some parents find themselves drawn to an opposite but equally devastating approach. The welcome is just that little bit *too* affectionate, as the same-sex parent consciously or unconsciously puts themself in direct competition. In effect, they say 'You may give yourself airs, but I am not yet ready to be retired from sexual attractiveness and can still best you at this game.' To the mortification of the son or daughter, the parent then uses all their considerable adult skills and charm to be more attractive to the boy or girlfriend than they are.

Of course, the fact that your sons and daughters have sexual equipment in working order and are aware of themselves as sexual beings, does not mean that they necessarily will want to use this potential. They often get conflicting messages from you. At first, warnings about the opposite sex, and then anxious enquiries if they don't have a close alliance with one of this dangerous group! Teenagers often find it very difficult to be just *friends* with a member of the opposite sex, because any liaison is immediately assumed to be romantic and sexual, and both come under pressure to make it other than it is. Teenagers can also become frightened and depressed if they don't have a boyfriend or girlfriend. They may become convinced that there is something wrong with them and that nobody will ever love them.

You might like to point out to them that the opposite sex are people, not things to own or be owned by, and that it is better to wait for a friendship that has real value than to grab at one just for the sake of it. They may need immense reassurance that people of their age group develop at very different rates, so rather than imitate their peers they should pay heed to what *they* need and want at the time. They also need to be reminded that a large amount of what they will be told by their peers is empty boasting. Many a young couple has been egged on by their 'friends', with tales of their prowess and experiences, to have intercourse. They then find that they are, in fact, the first in the group to lose their virginity – and often to become parents in one fell swoop!

Parents might look anxiously for a boy or girlfriend, even though they may not want to cope with the attendant disagreements, because it at least reassures them that their teenager is 'normal', and not homosexual. As I have already indicated, most young people experiment with members of their own sex, without this necessarily being their permanent sexual orientation. But the recent change in the law that lowered the age of consent for gay sex to eighteen (soon, perhaps, to sixteen in line with heterosexual age of consent) affects the fact that most boys who are going to find their sexual partners among their own sex are hardly likely to have a sexual moratorium in their teenage years.

Homosexual girls are still ignored in law, but our objections to either our sons or daughters falling in love with their own gender have little to do with legal niceties. Most parents will be devastated by the thought of discovering their son or daughter is gay. Partly, this is because it seems to be an attack on *your* sexuality – what does it say about you if your child chooses this form of sexual expression? Partly, it is the removal of a form of immortality. By turning away from heterosexual sex you see your child as refusing to give you grandchildren and refusing to carry on your family line. Partly, it is a deep-seated and unquestioning fear of the unusual and the different.

Parents might seek to turn their children against the idea of being gay by being violently critical or abusive about homosexuality. When they do discover the truth, they may seek to blame their offspring's conversion on another person who is seen as having corrupted their hitherto 'normal' child. In fact, although we don't know why some people are attracted to members of their own rather than the opposite sex, we do know that it is not something that can be induced by seduction. Neither is it a result of a hormonal imbalance that can be cured. Those who find their own sex equally attractive or more attractive than the opposite sex do so for the same reasons as some of us find blondes preferable to brunettes, or redheads sexier than both! Abuse does not change these feelings – it just ensures the young person comes to the realisation of their sexual orientation with fear, disgust and an often suicidally low self-esteem.

If one day your child is the apple of your eye, your hope for the future and the carrier of your family line, and the next day a disgusting 'queer' – what has changed? Not, certainly, the person themself, who is still the child who loves you and whom you loved. Only *your* perception of them. Which, then, is at fault – the person or your viewpoint, and which would be easier to change?

Young people should be able to express their sexuality. This is not to say that we should condone or encourage all levels of sexual *activity*. We should see, and help them to see, that sexual expression is not just one act – the act of sexual intercourse. It is a range of feelings and activities that stretches from the beginnings of self-awareness and exploration right through to complex sexual relationships with sexual intercourse. If we feel they are not yet ready to make the full journey, we would do better to allow them to take the first necessary steps, than to forbid them anything at all. If these first steps are made with confidence, and not tainted with guilt or fear, they are more likely to take their time and not to grab at experiences prematurely or inappropriately. The more we accept them and encourage them to accept themselves, the better chance they have of becoming caring, happy individuals able to make the loving and lasting relationships all parents want for their offspring.

5
THE BODY BEAUTIFUL

The self-absorption
of teenagers

'I hate my nose, and as long as I can remember I've wanted plastic surgery. Please don't tell me I'm being silly, because I know it is spoiling my life. I can't get friends because all they do is stare at it and make unpleasant jokes behind my back. I can't talk to my parents, and I'm sure my doctor would laugh at me. So can you tell me where to go for an operation? I'm only 16, but I do have some savings and I'm prepared to use them all.'

Letter to an agony aunt.

In the search for identity that dominates much of teenage years, appearance takes on a particular importance. Young people are often desperate to be 'normal', to fit in to the group they choose as their own and not to stand out as freakish or simply different. In spite of the fact that amongst adults they have a name for being rebels, within their own peer group, adolescents are un-yieldingly conformist. Those who enter puberty ahead or behind the majority can suffer agonies.

Your offspring may spend many hours considering what they have, what they can do with it and comparing it to everyone else. Adolescence is often spent in coming to terms with their own body and experimenting with clothes, make-up and jewellery and various forms of body adornment to conceal, reveal and make the most of the available material.

Teenagers live by comparison. They endlessly judge them-selves against the yardstick of their parents, their friends and the whole world. Tragically for them, the wider world has some pretty unfair tricks to play in this field. Many young people – and adults, too! – believe that there is such a thing as the Perfect Body. In women, this is slim, long-legged, tanned, hairless with perfectly formed up-thrust breasts. In men, it is also slim, tanned and long-legged, but has a proper sprinkling of hair in the appropriate places. Since no young person sees this parti-cular image in their mirror, they can become miserably con-vinced that not only are they falling short of the standard, but are positively handicapped. Despite the fact that they can see their bodies changing almost weekly, at any one time they are likely to despair that their undeveloped, half-finished form will stay that way for ever.

When they look at themselves in a mirror, it is as if all teenagers wore magnifying glasses. All young people notice and are concerned about themselves. For some, the concern is vague, faint and passes. For others it represents a major crisis. Teenage magnification enlarges any supposed defect until it fills the whole of the young person's vision. They are sure that nobody can possibly look at them or know them without stop-ping dead at this 'fault'. The size and shape of their body – their fat, their genitals, their nose and ears, their body hair, their skin with its stretch marks, moles, scars, acne and birthmarks, their body odour – all are sources of worry. Teenagers may take constant and even extreme measures to change or keep under control any of these aspects. We all had these worries when we were young, but often forget their intensity, even when faced with a miserable youngster. It might surprise most parents to know that a substantial number of teenagers are so unhappy about themselves that they seriously consider cosmetic surgery at some time and are only deterred by the thought that their parents and doctors would be unsympathetic and unhelpful.

According to one survey, three in five girls and a surprising one in five boys report having tried to lose weight. Puberty puts bulk on what might have been a spindly child's body and, in a society obsessed with diet and weight gain, very few teenagers manage to see this padding for what it is – the natural filling out of a pre-adult outline. But along with this padding, some teenagers do acquire an amount of unnecessary weight. In seeking to spend as much time as possible with their friends, teenagers can get into the habit of missing out on balanced meals in the family home and snacking on 'junk food' – most of which is high in sugars and fats and which encourages weight gain. Parents, in response to their teenagers pulling away, may place heavy emphasis on the importance of a shared meal. Not only will you start insisting that they be there, but you may go to great lengths to capture their interest with food you know they like. Surprise, surprise, these too are likely to lean heavily on rich ingredients. Eating can become an area of conflict. Food is often a lot more than just fuel for the body. Food is a reward for good behaviour. Food is an offering of love, and having it turned down is a keenly felt rejection. Food can even become a punishment.

We are all becoming far more health conscious and aware of the importance of a *sensible* diet. The word diet does not actually mean a strict regimen for losing weight. It means your usual intake of food. In the Western world, many of us have become used to a diet full of what are called 'empty calories' – too much sugar and fat that we don't need and that just converts to stores of excess body fat. We try to get rid of this by suddenly cutting down, hoping to make our bodies live off these fat reserves. Even if it does work, if we go back to our previous daily diet, the fat creeps back on. If most adults are confused and unhappy about the shape they are in, and how to deal with it, how much more difficult it is for young people, whose own efforts in this area are often directed or frustrated by the adult world.

Many teenagers become faddy over food in an attempt to pursue the Perfect Body. For some, the relationship between them and food takes on a particular significance. Anorexia nervosa – which means nervous loss of appetite – is known as the 'slimmers disease'. Both these descriptions are inaccurate.

Anorexia is not just a case of slimming gone too far, and very few anorexics cease to be hungry. Anorexia is an immensely complex psychological problem. Basically, it is about control. The normal fears and concerns of teenagers about their bodies become exaggerated, and the longing for both control of their bodies and their lives becomes intense and confused. One of the first and most obvious results of strict self-denial is that the body sheds much of its maturity and returns to being childlike. Girls can stop – or never start – menstruating, their body hair can become sparse and fine again and the padded hips, thighs and breasts of a woman may disappear. Boys, too, will lose muscle and return to being slight and smooth. The anorexic may exist in a constant state of raging hunger and be obsessed with food to the point of continually reading and talking about recipes and knowing the calorie content of every dish he or she may insist on cooking for the family. But they themselves will only pick and nibble. Their satisfaction comes from the triumph of subduing and controlling their own appetites, and denying you the power of being able to feed them. An anorexic is not someone who refuses the occasional meal or who complains about your cooking, but the one who has always 'just eaten' or is 'going to eat with friends'. It is the youngster who somehow is always about the kitchen but never sits down to a meal with you – or does, and then quickly exits to the bathroom (to vomit up the contents of his or her stomach, or to pass it in laxative-induced diarrhoea).

Anorexia is very rarely an individual problem, purely to do with the young person themself. It is more often a family problem, arising out of complicated conflicts between parents and child or parent and parent. It is more likely to arise in families where conflict simmers under the surface, than when discussions are open and honest. It is more likely to happen in families where great importance is placed on food and eating. This is not, I might add, the same as families who enjoy food. It also appears to occur when parents have high, unrealistic or rigid expectations of their children, or where mothers place a particular emphasis on their daughters, and themselves, remaining attractive and youthful. The two can be rivals to gain the attention of an often absent, or at least emotionally distant, husband and father, and it can lead to the daughter seeing refusing food as a way of both escaping her mother's control and becoming slim and beautiful.

Anorexic young people are often 'good', 'quiet', 'obedient' and 'compliant', and if your young people are anything but, at least heave a sigh of relief for small mercies!

The best way to deal with anorexia is not to get into the situation in the first place. The more you encourage your teenager to cope with the changes of adolescence, the less 'controlling' you are, the more realistic your demands on them, the more open and honest your disagreements and discussions, the less likely you are to have to face this problem. If it does arise, it is not an area in which to waste time feeling guilty or trying to assign blame. Young people in this situation desperately need their family to overcome their embarrassment and anger at what is going on and to seek professional help along with the sufferer, and to accept the advice and suggestions that would be offered.

As I've already discussed, the changes that occur in their bodies, particularly in the breasts and genital organs, can provoke very real fears in teenagers. They can view these changes not only with alarm, but guilt. Most young people masturbate, and most pick up the feeling that such activity is harmful, in spite of the fact of the overwhelming professional view that it is not only normal and natural but an essential part of development. Unable to discuss their behaviour, many teens get caught in a 'cause and effect' tangle. Because sexual excitement produces immediate changes such as the swelling of erectile tissue, the deepening of colour in various places and increased sensitivity, and these parts of the body also undergo similar permanent changes, many are sure that they have deformed themselves in the very way that the warnings given against such practices hinted they would. For that reason, they can be too inhibited to bring their worries to you or any other adult in authority, such as a doctor.

It is not only their sexual development that gives them cause for concern. While sitting staring at their mirror images, they often notice all sorts of things about themselves that create panic. Are their noses too big or too small? Have their chins an attractive shape? Do their ears stick out or their teeth protrude? What are those funny spots in front of their eyes, and do they herald early blindness? There are teenagers whose whole lives revolve around rigid body control; not smiling openly in case people stare and laugh at the gap in their teeth; not looking anyone straight in the eyes, in case people sneer at the funny bump in their noses; not moving their heads, in case their hair falls back to reveal a scar, a spot or a pair of Dumbo-like ears. Once formed and allowed to persist, this conviction that you are 'not quite right' can last for a lifetime. In most cases, the offending part is normal and the teenager needs no more than reassurance and understanding. But there *are* some instances when practical help could, and perhaps should, be offered.

We often feel that the best way to discourage young people from being so obsessed with their looks is to ignore them or belittle their concern. Often, it is more effective to listen and offer constructive advice.

Problems such as crooked, stained or protruding teeth can certainly be dealt with by a good dentist, on the National Health. Considering how important it is to be able to open one's mouth in front of people, you shouldn't feel that such treatment is a sign of vanity or a waste of anyone's time.

There are some surgical procedures that should wait until the patient is fully physically mature – noses, for instance are not usually operated upon for purely cosmetic reasons until the body is fixed in its outline at about 18 or 19. But protruding ears may be tackled earlier than that, even in childhood. Neither parents nor teenagers should feel unable to ask a doctor's advice and opinion early on – and it *is* to the family doctor you should go initially with these concerns, *not* to a private clinic or surgeon.

American and British society share a belief in the masculinity of body hair, rather than seeing it as a natural consequence of sexual maturity and a characteristic common to all human beings. For young men, it never grows darkly, thickly or quickly enough, and many will be concerned that their development is stunted and abnormal if they are late in producing 'ball hairs' or remain smooth-chested. In contrast, girls will be appalled at finding fine hairs around their nipples and in between their breasts, and ashamed at having growth on the legs, stomach and arms. Their belief in the ideal female form as being hairless is not helped by their memories of their former selves. Nor by the fact that nearly every image they see of women in our society, whether in art or advertising, presents the female body as smooth with no obvious and visible body hair. Nor by the multiplicity of means to remove and disguise female body hair offered to them.

There are many myths, that lead to unhappiness, surrounding depilation. Girls often respond to an early show of hair by shaving themselves. When they find the growth appears to become thicker and more profuse, they accept that it was the shaving that caused this, and add the resultant guilt to the misery of being 'abnormal'. In fact, there is nothing you can do to body hair to make it grow more quickly or to change its texture. If you could, you would make a fortune from all those boys despairingly trying to encourage a downy lip, and from men with bald patches! What actually happens is that young people start to notice their hair growth at just the time when it *is* becoming thicker, darker and more widespread. Subsequent hair growth will be more noticeable until the body has attained its natural adult distribution, and it will do this whether or not you depilate. But smoothing your body artificially can mean that you become hypersensitive to the new growth as it appears. Also, some methods of depilation can *seem* to coarsen the next growth of hair. If you pull out a hair by its root, the replacement strand will end up as the same colour, thickness and length, but in its early stages will appear finer and lighter. Shaving produces a stub with the same colour and dimension as the thickest part of the hair you have just cut off, and so appears coarser.

It is hardly practical to try to persuade young people to go against the tide of fashion of a whole culture. However, it would help if youngsters could understand that body hair on girls is hardly unusual, is thoroughly 'feminine' – and that any boy or girl who upsets them by saying otherwise is only showing their own painful ignorance.

Boys often take some time to show their growth and may not have as much of a thatch as they would wish. It may be instructive to point out that many male sex symbols are smooth-chested. There is nothing you can do to hurry along your son's moustache or chest hair.

For girls who would like to disguise their growth, it might be preferable to advise them on using bleach, depilatory creams or waxing than on shaving. The last might be cheaper, but it is a daily regimen that can make them feel awkward. Fair hair is always less noticeable than dark, so for facial and chest hair, bleach is likely to be the best solution. Depilatory creams are often the most convenient method, and waxing, although the most painful, gives the longest lasting result. If your daughter is old enough to worry about her appearance, she is old enough to use such products. She is less likely to make dreadful mistakes, and use a strong depilatory cream intended for the coarser skin of the legs on her tender face, or use household bleach or too strong peroxide instead of the proper cosmetic preparations available from a chemist, if she has had your support and guidance. You can also certainly reassure both yourself and her that employing any of these methods does *not* increase or strengthen hair growth, whatever anyone says to the contrary.

The skin, being the largest organ of the body, attracts more than its fair share of attention from the worried teenager. Acne is a perennial concern, and 'zits' probably account for more teenage jokes, harassment and angst than anything else. Teenagers spend millions of pounds every year on creams and lotions to hide or cure their spots. Most of these products only conceal, and do no more than take advantage of the transitory nature of even the severest bout of acne. At the worst, use of these products leads to picking, probing and constant rubbing of the site, encouraging the production of sebum – the skin's natural moisturising oil that is the main cause of the blocked pores that lead to spots.

Young people feel bad enough about spots without having to feel that they caused them. Prevalent myths are that the eating of fatty or sweet food, masturbating or having sexy dreams, not

washing, not exercising and not sleeping, all lead to spots. In fact, the only real cause of spots is being a teenager, and there's not much you can do about that except sit it out! Obviously a healthy lifestyle will make them look and feel more alert and fit, and will encourage their bodies to recover from any blemishes quickly, but even young world-class athletes at the peak of fitness can be zit-ridden, so it's nothing of which to be ashamed or worried. However, in some young people, acne can be so physically painful or disfiguring, or so emotionally disturbing that medical help should be sought.

There are over-the-counter preparations that a pharmacist can recommend, stronger than the normal, branded types. There is also a further level of treatment available from your own family doctor, who can prescribe creams or drugs to clear up or control attacks. In some cases, courses of antibiotics are recommended for either sex. For girls, various types of hormonal preparations can be extremely effective. She may be put on a pill very similar to the oral contraceptive or, indeed, on one of the many brands of contraceptive pill, without there being any ulterior motive for this medication on her part! In very bad cases, the family doctor may send his or her patient to a hospital skin specialist, either to clear up the acne, or for treatment on scar tissue left behind. Do remember that no reasonable GP who cares for his young patients would feel that a request for such help was a 'waste of time'.

The hormonal changes of adolescence can do more than pop up the odd spot. They can also lay down a network of fine lines that start off as red and then fade to a silvery white. These are most often found on the breasts, stomach, buttocks and thighs, and are usually known as 'stretch marks'. Stretch marks, or stria, are commonly found after a pregnancy or a considerable weight change. Many young people are shocked to find them, believing if they have experienced neither of these that it must be premature ageing. Stria are actually the result of bundles of fibres, located just under the skin, breaking apart. This can happen when the subcutaneous layer is stretched, or it can also be a reaction to hormone production, such as that experienced during adolescence. Since these bundles of fibres are *below* the skin, no amount of moisturising of the surface will have the slightest effect, and you cannot banish or prevent stretch marks with oils, creams, lotions or massage. The only way you can deal with them is to see them, not as a stigma but as a badge of adulthood. Be proud of your own stria, as being proof of the fact that you are not a plastic doll but a living, breathing human being – and make your offspring feel the same. You could also point out that the faint silvery tracks may seem as obvious as neon-lit highways to them, but be almost invisible to anyone else.

Using a sunbed to get a tan will not make stria fade. However, you may feel better about yourself in a bronzed state! Suntans are highly prized nowadays in both sexes and are often seen as a way of curing or covering up many imperfections. Some people, for instance, find that such treatment can clear up their acne. Do, however, remind your youngster that the greater your exposure, whether to natural sunlight or the sunbed, the more chance you have of developing a dry, tired skin, or even skin cancer, later in life.

Marks on the skin can embarrass and depress a lot of youngsters, especially during adolescence when they feel that their peer group will be scrutinising them and making judgements. Scars, birthmarks and even moles can be a source of anxiety and can prompt teenagers into trying a range of self-help remedies that can often be dangerous. Many will use wart-removing liquid, for instance, on moles, feeling them to be unsightly, especially if they are hairy. Moles are normally harmless, but damaging one might trigger off problematical changes and certainly harm the surrounding skin. Similarly, trying to cut out or otherwise alter scar tissue or skin blemishes is more likely to increase any unsightliness.

Medical techniques have advanced to the stage where much can be dealt with by a specialist, or even the family doctor in his or her own surgery. So, even if you think the birthmark or 'beauty spot' is charming or unnoticeable, it might make for a happier teenager if you were to find out how the young person themself felt, and encourage them to seek help if they would like it. You might also like to reassure yourself that if your teenager acquires a tattoo, from an illicit source before they are over the age of consent, or as soon as they are old enough to do so legally, this is not now irrevocable. New techniques mean that these, too, *can* be removed quite successfully when he or she finally decides to have this done.

The absorption in their bodies leads teenagers to experiment in a wide range of body adornment – clothes, make-up, jewellery and hair styling. Children copy adults in dressing up and inexpertly smearing make-up on their faces. During adolescence, the touch becomes more deft and expert as the youngsters deliberately pursue the effect they desire. Most body adornment seeks to emphasise their maturity as they begin to realise the power of physical attractiveness. Tight or revealing clothing that shows off the legs and breasts of a girl or the genital area or shoulders of a boy, all draw attention to their growing sexuality.

Most parents object to the clothes and, above all, the make-up on their young people. Partly, this objection is justified. In the early stages the teenager is likely to be lacking in subtlety and may indeed look tarty or simply ridiculous. However, parents should be aware of the fact that their reservations may have more to do with their own feelings, than with the actual image of the teenager in front of them. Your teenager is stating clearly that he or she is sexual – and it may not be the decibel level of the statement to which you object, but just the fact that it is being made at all! Make-up can trigger in you quite a disproportionate anger because, whether you openly realise it or not, you know the real meaning of paint on the face. Darkening our eyes and reddening our lips and cheeks mimics the dilated pupils and flushed skin of sexual excitement. We use make-up to attract the opposite sex by putting on the appearance of being aroused by them. Fathers particularly can be roused to uncomfortable anger at the sight of their little girls going outside the home in this state.

You may feel that your teenagers are putting out signals that can be misinterpreted. Their appearance could be taken by other teenagers and by adults as an open advertisement of sexual availability or aggressive intent. You may be right, and the body language they innocently display could indeed get them into trouble. However, in each succeeding generation, the significance of an item of clothing or a type of behaviour becomes softened. In Victorian days, a flash of ankle would be considered provocative. Some parents can still remember when ankle chains and fishnet tights were only worn by prostitutes – both are now unremarkable. Young people may indeed go 'over the top' in their experimenting. Where you think this could be misunderstood by others, you are likely to find your advice better accepted if you explain your objections and offer to help them achieve a better effect, than by deriding their attempts or forbidding them to display them.

Above all, you should recognise that most teenagers are not flaunting or offering their bodies in this display. They are practising its power and effect, and seeking assurance that they *are* attractive and acceptable. The more you criticise, the more they may be driven to wilder excesses to get *somebody's* admiration and approval, and the more they may realise the potential in their appearance as a weapon against you. How they dress and drape themselves, of course, indicates how they are feeling about themselves *at the time*. Safety pins through the ears or a mohican haircut are not signs that your son or daughter is heading for a life of brutalised hooliganism. They are still your lovely children under the new costume, and still need and deserve your love and approval. You, too, went through some pretty outlandish phases at their age. The fashions you wore may now seem innocent and staid, but to your parents they seemed as violently provocative as your teenagers' styles do to you!

When teenagers do get into a depression about themselves, and become convinced that they are fat, deformed or ugly, in the vast majority of cases it is their perception that is at fault, not the body itself. Their attitude is all-important, and self-esteem does not materialise out of thin air. However rebellious they may seem, and however often they may shout that they don't need you, it is their relationship with you that forms the foundation and the framework for their feelings about themselves and their dealings with the world. Your contribution to this is vital. If you have made, and continue to make, them feel loved, valued and of worth, they will be able to weather the complex conflicts of adolescence and to emerge from this period as rounded adults. Constant criticism, sarcasm, complaints or even rejection can only confirm them in extreme or destructive behaviour. After all, if you can never win, what's the point of competing? But a young person who is told that they succeed in holding your affection and interest, who knows that they are valued, will value themself and act accordingly. You have every right to object to some of their more bizarre experiments. But if you can make clear the distinction between disliking *what* they do and disliking *them*, they are far more likely to trust your opinion and come to you for advice and support.

What teenagers need most from their parents at this stage is their approval. Even if you don't like the wrapping, you should still show appreciation of the gift inside. If you *do* want to offer

criticism, remember that a touch of honey always makes it more *effective*. Saying 'Good grief, you look a mess. You're not going out like that,' is just asking for defiance. However, saying 'That looks fun. Mind you, I'm not sure it works as well as it could. How about trying . . .?' would put you in a far better position for offering constructive support rather than merely being destructive and making them defensive.

The balance between interfering and alienating a teenager, and offering support and winning their trust, is a fine one. Probably the best way to tread that narrow division is for you to take a deep breath before you say anything in criticism, and ask yourself quickly *why* you are about to say it. If you can put your own reactions through a mental filter each time, you can start to recognise when your impulses are going to be helpful, and when they may have exactly the opposite effect to the one you want. You will start to see when the help or hindrance you offer is from a genuine concern, and when it is prompted by a touch of envy or malice, or just from being out of touch.

6
WHAT'S YOUR POISON?

Tobacco, alcohol and illegal drugs

'I know she's been trying a few things, but whenever I try to talk to her about it she just says that I'm one to talk. Well, that's ridiculous, I mean you can hardly put the fact that I smoke and enjoy a glass now and again in the same league as taking drugs. If you can't tell the difference, then I think you're in a pretty bad way, but try telling that to her.'

John L.

Of all the experiments that teenagers can make, the area most parents fear is that of drug use. Even a pregnancy, we feel, could be dealt with or forestalled, but a drug addiction is seen as inflicting lasting or fatal damage. From the way the media portrays the problem, any parent would be forgiven for thinking that almost every teenager comes under pressure to try an illegal drug, and that most of them will do so. Without wishing to minimise the dangers of substances such as heroin, the fact is that *more* teenagers are damaged to a greater degree by alcohol abuse than by any form of illegal drug use.

We have a rather confused attitude to drugs in our society. Every culture has some substance – from fermented yak milk to magic mushrooms – that its citizens eat, drink or inhale in friendly situations to ease tension and promote sociability. In our culture, we use alcoholic drinks and tobacco, and these

97

materials are so much a part of our way of life that we do not think of them as 'drugs'.

Most of us have a fixed image of what a 'drug-fiend' will look like and behave. This is a dangerous stereotype, because it can blind us to the reality that anyone's father, mother, daughter, son or friend *can* become an addict to some substance or other, without appearing to be wild-eyed, scruffy or unpredictable. In focussing our attention on the illegal, we forget that many more lives are ruined or cut short by the effects of beer, spirits, wine or cigarettes than by heroin or cocaine. Furthermore, to a young person who is questioning society's attitudes, the difference between getting drunk and getting 'stoned' may be seen as just a question of adult hypocrisy.

Before you consider illegal drugs therefore, it is necessary for you to look at the substances you buy and use yourself. Most of us see nothing wrong in taking 'a little wine for thy stomach's sake and thine often infirmities', as the Bible has it. Many of our social occasions are built around the offering of alcohol. Whether at home or in public, we often feel that friendliness, generosity and hospitality are shown in the offer of a drink or a cigarette. A refusal is seen as a rejection of all these kind impulses.

We drink and smoke for many other reasons, too. A cigarette and a pint not only have symbolic power, they both also relax you physically, and many of us enjoy the effects. Even if you would describe yourself as a light or non-drinker, it is highly unlikely that your youngsters could reach their teenage years without being steeped in this common attitude towards alcohol and tobacco. Drinking the product of grape, fruit or grain, and inhaling the smoke from burning leaves is something that normal, friendly grown ups do in their normal, friendly grown up gatherings. Which means that if a trainee adult wants to demonstrate their friendliness, normality and maturity, the best thing to do is to order a drink and a packet of cigarettes!

Some parents try to protect their youngsters from the possible dangers of drinking or smoking by bribing them, or forbidding them to experiment. Both methods have their drawbacks. Forbidding an activity instantly makes it doubly glamorous and enticing. By stressing that a certain act should not be done 'until you are over 16/ over 18/ over 21/old enough', you set up a desirable goal. If drinking and smoking are things real adults do, then the reverse is true – start drinking and smoking and you show yourself as having passed a rite of passage and attained adulthood. Offer a ready-made rule to break to a questioning adolescent, and any youngster worth their salt will leap at the challenge! Bribery invites corruption. With no reason to keep away from drink or tobacco beyond the desire to earn the reward, most people could be persuaded to dabble and lie. So, bribery can actually encourage the practice of deceit.

A better method is to examine *why* we use drugs, how they can effect us and whether these effects are actually worthwhile. Apart from the symbolic meaning and the physical effects, many of us also indulge for a range of emotionally satisfying reasons. Even adults will sometimes try a new drink to be daring or fashionable, and young people particularly will want to experiment, to be rebellious and to go against your rules. Illegal drug use can then seem especially exciting in that it offers a heightened experience of *all* these areas.

Unfortunately, just knowing about drugs may not be enough. Intelligent, sensible young people who go through extensive health education at school and who know all about the dangers of tobacco, can still start smoking cigarettes. We abuse substances for reasons that have nothing to do with sense, logic or knowledge. It may be because of peer-group pressure – everyone else is drinking, smoking or shooting up and we don't want to stand out as different. It may be because of emotional pressures – life is getting on top of us, and a quick slurp, drag or fix will make us feel better. Just talking about the dangers of these substances cannot in itself prepare us to resist the pressures from outside and inside. The only way to do that is to discuss the pressures as well, to acknowledge how they affect us and to work out ways of avoiding and resisting them.

At the moment, we tend to use the bogeyman syndrome in talking about drug use. By this, I mean that we *only* tell young people about the horror stories. We tell them that drugs will harm them, destroy them, impoverish and degrade them. We don't dare mention the reason people use drugs – because they can make you feel good – in case that sends them off to give it a try. This approach is fine, if they never encounter a drug or a drug taker. However, if they meet someone who appears sane, well and in control and who offers them 'a taste' that *does* have a nice effect, and *doesn't* harm them immediately, they may conclude that you were lying. Since you didn't say it would feel so good, you obviously don't know what you are talking about, and *nothing* you have said is worth remembering.

If you don't discuss the whole package, you risk having the essential bits thrown out. It *is* possible to know, for instance, that using 'crack' is probably the best physical sensation you are ever likely to experience – and yet have *no* intention of ever trying it. If you want your teenager to stay off drugs, it's better that they learn from *you* that what is offered is short-term pleasure followed by long-term trouble, than hear the threats from you and the promises from someone else, and opt to believe only the latter. The more you know about the subject, the better you can understand the temptations your teenager may come up against. You can then prepare them to resist, or be alert yourself to the tell-tale signs.

Drug use seems to go in fashionable cycles. 'Speed', or amphetamines, cannabis and LSD were the favoured drugs of the sixties and seventies. The eighties have seen a rise in the use of heroin and cocaine. International practices dictate what is available, and economics dictate what is used. Cocaine, for instance, tends to be a 'yuppie' drug, not only because it is clean and easy to use, but because it is expensive. Heroin, once a very pricey habit, has come down-market. Speed appears to be making a comeback in Britain today and has been dubbed the 'young man's or poor man's cocaine', since it is one sixth the price of the real thing. Cannabis is still the most favoured substance among illegal drug users today, but amphetamines, manufactured in illicit laboratories, are now the next most popular drug.

The use of illegal drugs has its own language and rituals. These serve two purposes. Users can talk about their scene without the uninitiated understanding their cryptic comments. The rituals add to the mystique and excitement of what is going on. Unfortunately, there is a side effect, in that young people can often be drawn in, not just because of the glamour, but from sheer ignorance. Being invited to take a 'hit of smack' sounds infinitely less threatening than an offer of a dose of heroin.

What is wrong with using drugs? A strange question perhaps, but one that needs answering. Various drugs affect you in different ways. All have mind-altering properties and make you calm or excited, happy or elated – that is why we use them. But at the same time, some exert other influences, such as increasing your risks of developing certain forms of cancer, or damaging your heart, liver or other organs in your body. Most are addictive. Addiction is when your body needs regular doses of a substance or else reacts in various unpleasant ways.

Most drugs that are addictive also create what is called tissue tolerance. This is when you become accustomed to a drug and need an increased input to achieve the same effect. In some cases, an addiction is emotional rather than physical. That is, the body can function, but the user feels unable to face real life without the support of whatever drug they are taking. Some of this can be said of the illegal drugs we fear, such as heroin and cocaine. It can also be said of such items as tobacco, alcohol, tea and coffee!

Both alcohol and tobacco cause damage – tobacco in any quantities and alcohol if consumed regularly in amounts over a surprisingly low limit. The professional opinion is that a man drinking more than 20 units of alcohol (for example, 10 pints of beer or 20 small spirits) and a woman drinking more than 13 units regularly each week, could be putting their own and their family's health at risk. Women are advised to drink less than men because the difference in size and metabolism generally means that they have a lower tolerance for alcohol. Unfortunately, this also applies to young people. The immature body builds up tolerance and becomes addicted more quickly on a smaller amount than does the mature body.

Addiction is a problem, whether it is to legal or illegal drugs, but stepping outside the law for your kicks can bring problems in addition to the obvious ones. You cannot guarantee the dosage or the purity of a drug that is sold on the streets. Many of these are adulterated or 'cut' with substances which can sometimes in themselves be harmful. Or addicts can die from an overdose when a 'fix' is unexpectedly pure and therefore much stronger than usual. When injecting, the user may not be able to entirely dissolve all the drug or its additives in a solution and find themselves developing dangerous or fatal abscesses or blood clots. Lack of sterile conditions can lead to the same results. Since many users 'shoot up' in company and share needles, hepatitis and HIV, the virus that can cause AIDS can be passed round along with the drug.

The illegal or abused substances with which your teenager might come into contact are heroin, cocain, LSD, Ecstasy, amphetamines, barbiturates, tranquillisers, solvents and cannabis. However, drugs are continually appearing, disappearing and reappearing as new variations are discovered or made available and as the economics of the drug market make today's expensive, yuppie-taste available to everyone or puts the price up on yesterday's cheap thrill. All are available for a price in even the most out-of-the-way spot in this country, and drug use is no longer just a city problem.

Heroin is the drug that probably causes most alarm, possibly because the way it was once taken requires a definite commitment. Heroin can be 'mainlined' or injected, and the obvious fear is that once a youngster has gone far enough to be willing to stick needles in himself, they must be well and truly hooked. This may no longer be true. Heroin can, in fact, be smoked – a process called 'chasing' or 'chasing the dragon'. Instead of being dissolved in heated water and injected into a vein (mainlining) or just under the skin (popping), the talc-like powder, which can be any colour from white to dark brown, can be heated on a piece of tinfoil until it partially melts and gives off fumes. Chasing the dragon is so called because the melted powder forms mercury-like balls that have to be pursued with a straw or rolled tube of paper. The powder can also be 'snorted' or inhaled through the nose.

Heroin is known by many names – 'H', 'scag', 'shit', 'smack', 'horse', 'blow' or 'jones' are some of the most common. Getting addicted actually requires quite a bit of effort. The first experience is most unlikely to be pleasant, but to lead to nausea and vomiting. Only after a few times will the user experience the main goal – the 'rush', or sudden, almost sexual, feeling of euphoria and pleasure. This usually lasts for a few minutes, to be followed by a period of several hours of relaxation and contentment.

After a period of use, someone on heroin will build up the form of immunity that is called 'tissue tolerance'. Not only does the user need larger and more frequent doses to achieve an effect, but the pleasurable element diminishes. Worst of all, the body begins to need the drug to remain in a reasonably normal state. If the drug is not taken, the user goes into withdrawal and suffers a range of uncomfortable symptoms such as chills, cramps, nausea and itching.

Heroin is usually sold in 'wraps'. These are very small packets of folded paper, and the current cost can be as low as a few pounds a dose. To inject heroin, the necessary equipment would be a supply of water in which to dissolve the powder, a heat source such as a candle or matches, a spoon or tin lid in which to 'cook' the mixture, a syringe or a dropper with a needle attached with which to inject or 'pop', and a tie, belt or cord with which to cut off the circulation and raise a vein in an arm or leg. You don't even have to inject yourelf. Some addicts use friends or pay others to do this for them, so being afraid of needles is no protection. 'Chasing' would only require a heat source and tinfoil or a lid.

Cocaine is a far less messy drug, but often attracts elaborate use. The fine, crystalline white powder is often 'snorted'. It is spread upon a mirror, divided with a knife or razor into 'lines' and sniffed up through tubes of paper, straws or from custom-made little spoons. Cocaine, also known as 'coke' or 'snow', gives an even greater rush than heroin. Heroin makes you dozy and calm, but cocaine gives instant energy and is often used to increase the enjoyment of making love or music. Cocaine is widely used by creative people. It has been argued that cocaine does not addict its users in the same way as heroin, and certainly users *can* take it or leave it without physical side effects. However, the 'crash' or 'down' after a cocaine high can be so depressing, and users can have a strong enough aversion to coming down, that they may as well be physically dependent.

Cocaine can also be dissolved and injected. Cocaine can also be processed into a crystaline form called crack. Crack is sold in 'rocks' that are smoked and that give an immediate 'rush' that is said to be the most intense of all drug sensations. Because its intensity is so short-lived, it can prompt repetitive use that can lead to a form of addiction within days.

LSD (D-lysergic acid diethylamide) is also known as 'acid', and was a favourite hippie drug of the sixties which is now becoming popular again. It is a liquid, and is sold soaked into small pieces of paper, in aspirin-sized or tiny pills or, now rarely, in gelatine. These are known respectively as 'blotter acid', 'tab acid', 'microdots' and 'windows'. LSD is an hallucinogenic, giving the user visions and a sense of wide understanding for a period of time called a 'trip'. Acid is not addictive, but it does produce very unpredictable results. Good trips may be very pleasant and inspiring, but a bad trip can be a nightmare. Either can be replayed later in 'flashes' that last for a few minutes to several hours, and that can occur weeks or even months after the acid was actually taken or 'dropped'. Acid users may feel depressed afterwards, and some can react with panic and long-lasting or even permanent mental instability. However, professional opinion is that the drug does not impose such a reaction, but only allows it to emerge in someone already predisposed.

Ecstasy, known as E but technically called MDMA, is an unusual drug that acts both as an hallucinogenic and as an amphetimine. It's a drug particularly associated with raves and dancing and is available in pill form. Users say they experience tingling sensations and that normal feelings become intensified but without the hallucinations that can come with LSD. Body temperature can rise and while users can have feelings of well-being and happiness – hence the name – confusion, paranoia and anxiety have all been reported and there have been deaths associated with this drug. MDMA is not physically addictive, although tolerance to it can be built up.

Pills are often the easiest drugs to obtain, in a society where some doctors still hand out repeat prescriptions for Valium, Librium and other tranquillisers without counselling their patients. Your son or daughter may not have to buy a supply from a dealer, but can take it for free from your own medicine cabinet.

Tranquillisers, which relieve anxiety and inhibitions, are called 'downers'. Amphetamines, which make you feel alert and full of well-being, are called 'uppers'. These are available in tablet form or as capsules, and some of those sold on the black market are known as 'dexies', 'purple hearts', 'blues', or 'black bombers'.

Methylamphetamine, or 'meth', and amphetamine sulphate, commonly known as 'speed', are also sold as a powder, to be dissolved and injected, or sniffed. Mandrax and Quaaludes, 'mandies', were a popular downer in the sixties and seventies, but have now largely been replaced by the barbiturates and benzodiazepines – Valium, Librium, Ativan and others. Whether in legal or illegal use, all these 'uppers' and 'downers' can create both psychological and physiological dependence. They are also dangerous as most can produce an overdose if misused, sedating or exciting the system to excess, especially if taken with alcohol.

One of the newest, cheapest and easiest 'highs' is achieved by sniffing solvents. Glue, hair spray, nail varnish, paint stripper, lighter fuel, aerosols and correcting fluid all contain substances that give euphoria, excitement and even hallucinations that last for between five minutes and a few hours. Short-term side effects are headaches, drowsiness, irritability and memory loss. Long-term effects can be brain damage, liver or kidney failure, leukaemia, anaemia and degeneration of the nervous system. If, that is, the sniffer does not die while sniffing, from respiratory failure or heart attack. Sniffers inhale straight from the container, or squirt the substance into a plastic or paper bag to place over the mouth and nose, to be 'huffed' or inhaled. As well as smears of glue or the odour of the solvents, a sniffer can often be noticed by a cluster of sores or spots around the mouth.

Cannabis has become one of the most controversial drugs, since many people feel it should be made legal. Cannabis, or marijuana, comes from the hemp plant, which can be grown in Britain but is usually imported. It is available as a resin or gum (a dark brown material), as an oil or as the dried leaves and stalks. It is usually smoked. The oil or resin is combined with tobacco, while the leaves can be unmixed. The material is rolled in cigarette papers, into a 'joint', although it can be burnt in specially made small pipes. Cannabis has many names – 'Mary Jane', 'Mary Warner', 'hash', 'ganja', 'weed', 'grass', 'shit', 'dope' and 'pot' are just a few. It is not addictive in itself, and although it may have harmful effects on the brain and body, these have not been proved conclusively, and would appear to be less than those associated with either alcohol or tobacco.

However, while cannabis *is* illegal, it carries a particular risk if used by young people. That is, that its use can form an introduction into the drug sub-culture. The excitement of doing something forbidden, the thrill of belonging to an apparently exclusive, outlaw group, the mystique of using the language and paraphernalia peculiar to drug use, can all become more important and enticing than the drug itself. Indeed, young people often dabble in all the trappings of the drug culture – wearing the clothes and using the slang – without actually advancing into substance abuse. They can do this for the thrills it affords or to be part of something they feel is attractive, or just to get a rise out of you! However, there are powerful criminal financial interests involved even at the very lowest level of drug dealing. This makes your teenager a valuable asset, and should he or she accept the first free or cheap taste, they are likely to be pressured into becoming customers.

Drug taking can be expensive in many ways. A small habit can swallow up pocket money, allowance and earnings, and can grow into a bottomless hole that demands the proceeds of theft, prostitution or drug dealing itself. Future careers or jobs can be blighted, not only because the young person becomes too concerned with getting supplies to bother about school, college or work, but because involvement with the police can give them a criminal record that deters potential employers.

When it comes to drugs and their use, it is important for you to get the various substances into perspective. All drugs are not the same, and there is a world of difference between cannabis and heroin, their effects and their dangers. If you waste your fear and anger on the former, you can run the risk of minimising the dangers of the latter, another instance of the 'bogeyman syndrome'. Promise dreadful retribution for both pot smoking and mainlining, and if your teenagers find that the sky does not fall after a few furtive joints, they may well be tempted to try a bit of chasing. Just as the odd dram does not lead everyone to become a hopeless alcoholic, so some experiments in drug use do not lead on to hard or regular use.

The key to keeping your teenagers off drugs is in being able to discuss and explain the facts honestly and without hysteria, and in not giving them the reasons for seeking escape into drugs. If you answer their questions ahead of time, they are less likely to dip a toe out of curiosity. If, however, they are tempted, it helps to know what to look for so that you can give early help. It's no good ignoring your suspicions and leaving intervention until the youngster has a well-established habit.

One of the great dilemmas drug availability has thrust upon

parents is how to judge when to trust and when to intervene. On the whole, it is essential for young people to be able to know that their rooms are private territory. Nothing is quite as unsavoury and contemptible as the parent who snoops around their son's or daughter's papers and belongings. However, if you have a *genuine* fear that they might be doing something that could seriously damage their health and put their lives at risk, you might feel that this justifies a search.

Some of the obvious first signs are seeing the objects associated with drug use in your teenager's possession. Scorched tinfoil, spoons with a bent handle, charred tin lids or bowls, mirrors and razor blades, screws of paper, discarded tins or bottles of solvents, cigarette papers, eye droppers, or pill bottles (especially when you know he or she has not been to the doctor recently for a legitimate reason), all should make you ask for a discussion. Another worrying sign would be spatters of blood in the bathroom or in your teenager's room or on their clothes, especially on the arms or legs. Mainlining leaves 'tracks' or puncture marks around the injected vein, and the young person who flatly refuses to roll up their sleeves or wear brief clothing in summer could be sending out strong messages to you.

However, you might only see these signs if your teenager actually wants you to do so. He or she could find it difficult to start a dialogue, and leave tell-tale traces to prompt you to speak out. Just as often, the young person will hide any evidence, and it is only a change in their behaviour that might show that something is wrong. The main problem here is that many of the signs of drug taking are not that different from the classic mood swings and physical ups and downs of adolescence. You may have to be particularly sensitive and alert to separate the 'normal' bloody-mindedness of a teenager from the desperate instability of the regular drug taker. If your teenager suddenly becomes exceptionally moody, swinging from being sunny tempered to being sulky, or shows unexpected bad temper or aggression, this should cause concern. Other signs may include a change in appetite. He or she may stop eating or suddenly have cravings for sweet things. The teenager might alter sleeping patterns, staying up for all hours and never seeming to go to bed, or becoming impossible to shift in the morning. Old friends may be dropped, and study or work as well as sports and other interests might go by the board. New friends could appear mysteriously, and your teenager might suddenly start taking phone calls or visits at odd times of the day or night, and insist on going out immediately. They may become furtive, secretive and tell obvious lies, and money or belongings, their own and yours, could melt away.

If you do see any of these signs, the first of the Golden Rules is *don't panic*. You might be mistaken about their significance and an hysterical accusation is more likely to push your youngster towards anti-social or self-destructive behaviour. You and your partner, or a good friend, need to focus your feelings and attitudes first, to get the situation into perspective. Drug use is not necessarily a one-way trip to the cemetery. In spite of the horror stories, hardly any drugs are impossible to come off – barbiturates, where the withdrawal symptoms in a heavy user can be life-threatening, are probably the only exception. In all other cases, the withdrawal period or 'cold turkey', when the body has to readjust and get accustomed to being without the drug, can be unpleasant, but short-lived and tolerable. Withdrawal from heroin addiction, for instance, with its cramps, chills and runny nose, is actually no worse than a bad bout of 'flu. The difference is that the addict knows relief is just a fix away, and the person who seeks escape from the real world in drugs is likely to be the sort of person who will be unwilling to endure the temporary pains of cold turkey.

Getting someone off drugs requires three steps:

1. For them to decide to make that commitment.
2. For them to go through withdrawal.
3. For them to find life exciting or interesting without drugs.

You can't *make* a teenager who is using drugs turn their back

on their artificial contentment or appeal. All you can do is to help
them find something better, resolve the problems that led them
to take drugs in the first place and to make that decision for
themself. Spending thousands of pounds drying them out, and
then returning them to the life or environment that tipped them
into drug use in the first place, is just a good way of wasting
energy and money. There are some excellent specialist agencies
that can advise and support you and your family if drugs are your
problem. Most young people *don't* get pulled into this trap, but the
parents of those who do are not alone and can find sympathetic
guidance, both from professionals and from self-help groups.

If you want to be sure that your teenager is unlikely to turn to
drugs, there are some strategies you can adopt. They mainly
consist of removing the *reasons* for drug taking – a wish to
escape, boredom or a desire to rebel. Young people who are
loved and feel confident in their parents' approval, are less likely
to need drugs. Young people who have a good self-image are
more likely to hold out against the threats, sneers or blandish-
ments of their friends. Young people who are involved in activities – whether social, sporting or academic – have less need for
such an escape. Young people who can talk over their disagreements with their parents and the adults around them can
show their revolutionary tendencies in less destructive ways.

The other area is for you to avoid demonstrating the appeal of
mind-altering substances. There is little point in giving out
moral statements on the perils of drugs if you come home in the
evening and sink into the sofa with a loud sigh and a gin and
tonic or a beer. Do you make jokey comments about guests who
refuse drinks, or are you always ready to offer a non-alcoholic
alternative? Do you smoke, and have you ever taken pills to tide
you over a crisis? It isn't the usage that will push your young
people towards a drug lifestyle, but whether or not you are
prepared to discuss the part these substances play in your life,
and how you see them. As with so much in parenting, love, care,
honesty and discussion are the lifebelts that keep you and your
adolescents safe from drowning.

7
FAMILY CRISIS

A strategy for coping with problems

'It's funny, but before the marriage Sylvia's son seemed such a great kid and we really got on quite well. But I suppose all teenagers go through phases and he certainly is going through one now – he cheeks me all the time and he argues with his mother and is not doing so well at school. I know a new father must be difficult for him, but he seemed to like the idea and he didn't have any objections before. So I don't think that's the reason he's being difficult now.'

Jack T.

By its very nature, adolescence is a time of turmoil. Teenagers will be testing themselves and their relationships, and there may be frequent, almost routine, arguments and discussions both within the family and between them and their friends and contacts. However, the turmoil can be intensified if something drastic happens to affect the family as a whole – an internal crisis or one imported from outside. The break up of the family through separation or divorce; the death of a relative or friend; the remarriage of a parent and the arrival of a step family; the birth of a new brother or sister, or the marriage of an existing one; a change of lifestyle forced by a move of house or a new job for parents – or the loss of one – all can have profound effects on the young person. Such changes can prove difficult at any time of life, but they may have greater significance to a young person during adolescence.

Very few families get through the adolescent years without some major life change of this type. How you deal with your own worries and how you communicate with your teenager can mean the difference between this being an uncomfortable period they can weather, and one that places upon them an unmanageable burden. Parents in crisis often protect young people from what we see as the painful stresses of adult life. Not only do we try to shield them from the event itself – delaying telling them that grandfather's illness *is* fatal, or that you are coming to the decision to end your marriage – but we hide our subsequent responses. They have enough to bear, we reason, without coping with the shock of seeing their strong, all-knowing parents breaking down in confusion or grief. The last thing we wish to show is that we are weak, worried or afraid, for that might make them totally insecure.

The result is often the opposite of that which you intended. If you have succeeded in hiding the situation from your teenagers, they will then assume that there is no problem and you are either exaggerating or being silly. They will go about their business in blithe unconcern, scraping your nerves raw. In fact, hardly any young people are this blind. They know full well that something is up, and are more likely keenly to resent your treating them 'as children'. Or, far from being reassured by your apparent strength, they will conclude that you don't give a damn that grandpa is dead, or dad has gone. They may find it impossible to come to you for comfort. How could they, if you so obviously do not share their grief? They may even blame you for the situation. If you aren't upset it happened, they will reason you might have caused it deliberately.

We all react to a crisis, such as a death, with a complex rush of feelings. The circumstances of the death, and our relationship with the dying person before the event, fill us with all sorts of emotions. We may feel disbelief that someone we saw up and about the day or week before is never going to walk through the door again. We may feel guilt, wishing we had been kinder, more helpful and that we had shown our love more openly. We may also feel anger at the person, for leaving us and being the cause of such unhappiness. Our anger could also be directed at the world, for continuing as if nothing had happened, and at everyone around us, for seeming to be so unconcerned. Worst of all, we may hate ourselves, for having such dreadful thoughts. We may go into a state of shock, when nothing makes sense and everything is seen through a haze. And we may be seized with an awful fear that we or other members of the family could also die very soon.

Most of us share these reactions to any serious crisis, but not necessarily at the same time. These emotions can be so powerful, uncomfortable and unexpected, that we may try to hide or deny them, not only to others, but also to ourselves. Adolescents, struggling to cope with the other conflicting passions of their age, are all the more likely to retreat behind a barrier of studied indifference. Both sides might misinterpret each others' reactions. You may, for instance, take silence to mean a lack of concern or an admirable strength, when in fact it conceals a screaming hurricane of guilt and terror. By misinterpreting their feelings, you may deal with them in an inappropriate way – and they, you. The result can be friction at exactly the time when you all need each other's support and understanding.

Just because young people have not accumulated that much experience of life, does not mean they cannot understand what is going on, or that they will not feel profound grief and despair. In fact, it often means that they feel it more keenly. Unlike adults, who have been through bad times and so know that eventually you do feel better, young people have no way of anticipating the fading of this awful pain. Whatever you may say in comfort, they are sure that such agony will never pass. You can look back half a lifetime and remember a crisis of 15 to 20 years ago, and be reassured by the fact that you survived it. Half a lifetime to a teenager is measured in years, not decades, and a few months seems an eternity.

We tend to take teenage moods fairly lightly. Adolescents spend so much time going into apparently deep depressions – which are often hormonally produced blue moods or impulsive and short-lived responses to arguments with friends – that we often miss the transition to a genuine and longer lasting misery. An extra crisis can be the final straw to an already overwrought teenager, and they can slide into the paralysing grip of real depression.

Full-blown depression is characterised by lethargy, inertia and a carelessness about appearance and well-being. Of course, it is not always easy to spot when these are the symptoms of a real problem since all young people can go through stages of being apparently lazy, slatternly and sullen. We sometimes feel that only adults are capable of feeling true despair, and that a suicide threat from a 'child' is silly, hysterical or merely attention-grabbing. The last may be true. There is no better way to focus attention than by killing oneself. Alas, such threats are often anything but silly, in that the threateners can and do carry out their intention. Sometimes, suicide attempts that were supposed to make you take notice of their unhappiness, 'fail'. That is, instead of just frightening you, they bring about a death. But frequently, a young person's suicide bid is deadly serious, and is done with the full intention of removing them from what they see as an intolerable situation.

When a young person threatens to kill themselves, or starts 'saying farewell' in obvious ways, it is time to sit up and take notice. Forget the myth that those who threaten never do – a high proportion of people who kill themselves give clear warnings beforehand. Having received despairing letters from many young people whose threats and attempts to kill themselves have been dismissed as 'mere attention-grabbing', and who have been punished and told off rather than helped or comforted, I feel that we should re-examine our attitudes towards such behaviour. Why should a young person *not* be given attention? Does being shown you are loved and cared for spoil you in any way? Selfish or arrogant behaviour is found more often in

neglected children that in those given affection and considera-
tion. If this is the only way a young person can call for someone
to look at them and listen to them, it is a pretty sad reflection on
what has happened in the family up to that point. When we
dismiss such desperation, how far are we hitting out as a means
of salving our own guilt at letting it get this far?

Another 'attention-getting device' is open sexual activity, or
even pregnancy. This can certainly provoke a family crisis of its
own, but more often than not it appears to come on top of the
problems with which you are already struggling. You may well
be tempted to wash your hands of a teenager who is so selfish as
to give you one more burden, not understanding that it could
well be their difficulty in coming to terms with family problems
that has prompted their action in the first place.

Young people often initiate or allow a sexual relationship
when they feel invisible at home – unloved, uncared for, or just
set aside by parents who are too bound up in their own difficulties or interests to spare time for them. One way of grabbing
your attention in no uncertain terms is to leave evidence of a
sexual relationship – a packet of contraceptive pills, a packet of
condoms or a diary with explicit entries – lying around where

you are sure to find it. They may even deliberately risk pregnancy, seeing it as a way of holding a partner and perhaps
starting with them their own, idyllic, family that they imagine
will shelter them. Or, they see a baby as a possible source of
unfettered love, and also of status. Pregnancy is also a way of
making parents unmistakably aware of the fact that they are no
longer small children – becoming, or getting a girl, pregnant is
an acknowledged 'adult' action.

Alternatively, young people can express their anger and confusion in behaviour that up to then has been foreign to them,
such as stealing, joy-riding, drug taking, vandalism or fighting.
They may break up with old friends who are unable to understand or help cope with what is going on, and seek out other
young people in a similarly 'deprived' situation. When faced
with an outsider concerned with this behaviour, such as a
teacher, social worker or member of the police force, it can be
tempting for parents to deny that their youngster could have
been involved. Such a response rarely shows unconditional love
and trust in the teenager, but a wish to defend your own position
and evade the real issue. It's not a question of taking an outsider's word against that of your child, or of letting them down; if
they are behaving in an anti-social and uncharacteristic way,
they need your help both to face up to this fact and to sort out
what is going on.

The main difficulty that parents encounter is that the crisis
itself takes most of your attention and energy, leaving very little
time for you to spend puzzling out your teenager's complicated
responses and how to deal with them. If you are trying to come to
terms with a death or the break up of your marriage, it can be
virtually impossible to see past your own feelings and to put
yourself in your teenager's shoes. Even worse, there can be
situations that spell disaster for them that, in fact, are highly
exciting for you – a move to a new house or job, or a new member
of the family. In such a case, you may not have even realised that
you *were* in the middle of a family crisis!

One of the most difficult, but nowadays most common,

dilemmas, is how to cope with the introduction of a step parent, and often their own children, to yours. You may think that any fatherless or motherless child would welcome a new parent. Think again! However much more comfortable you think it will be to have a 'proper' family again, and however kind or loving the new parent and their family, step relationships are almost invariably troublesome, at least at first. You may have got over the loss of your former partner, but children can very rarely shrug off the loss of a parent. While spouses can be replaced, mothers and fathers cannot. The presence of this new adult can be seen as an insult to the lost parent. You can't have loved them as much as you pretended if you are this willing to turn your back on their memory. It is also an insult to the young person concerned – since you are rejecting the memory of *their* father or mother, might you also be willing to put them aside in due course?

Children in a one-parent family have one advantage in that they have the undivided attention of the remaining parent, and they often pride themselves on the responsibility they are given and the support they give. A new parent removes this exclusive relationship. A new family also gives them rivals who invade their territory, or upon whom they are imposed. Both sides will wind up feeling as if they have been made second best, and the other children given special privileges.

Step families give children unique problems, whatever their age, but teenagers often find it hardest to cope. Just at the time when they are learning to be independent of their family and beginning the long, hard task of breaking away, their secure foundation is shaken. You can only step out on your own successully if you are sure that what you are leaving is safe – safe in your absence, and safe for your return. When teenagers spread their wings, it is not with the intention of flying off and never coming back. The process is full of little 'training flights', in which they launch out, and just as quickly return, to ask for your approval and comments.

If the family they are breaking away from is in upheaval,

leaving becomes fraught. They become terrified of doing anything to upset what appears to be a precarious balance, in case a
push from them brings the whole thing down. Such teenagers
become our idea of 'good' teenagers – quiet, unassuming and
obedient. Or, looked at another way, clinging and incomplete,
for how can they ever learn to be independent adults if they are
too afraid to start now? Alternatively, they may go into a frenzy of
rebellious activity, in an effort to see whether the past break-up
or death was their fault, and they can make it happen again. The
first group, the 'goodies', may never completely establish their
own separate identities. The latter may start far too early and
make their break, either in spirit or in body, before they have
even finished growing up.

Young people need predictability and assured continuity, and
so are certainly going to be hurt by any drastic change in their
lifestyle. If you try to keep awareness of an impending change
from them as long as possible, you might buy yourself a few
months or even a few years of peace – at the cost of their being all
the more damaged by the eventual event. The damage will be
greater because they had no time to prepare, and because they
will also have to cope with the awful realisation you have
deceived them.

Teenagers, for all their bohemian behaviour, want just as
much security from their parents as do small children, and are
often most upset at any hint of your wanting to kick over the
traces. But, even more than young children, they want consistency of attitude and truth from you. No young person, however
innocent and unworldly, is insensitive to the ebb and flow of
your emotions and behaviour. Very few are unable to see when
something in the family is not quite right. It is not reality that
spoils their innocence, but cynicism and disillusionment. These
are brought about more surely when they have to face the
hypocrisy and pretence of the adult world, than when they are
given the honest truth.

Teenagers are well able to cope with unpleasant facts if they
are presented in a straightforward fashion, by the people they

trust and care for most. You can enlist their help and invite their understanding by telling them what is bothering you, or what might be about to happen to you all, in a round-table discussion. You may find it surprisingly helpful, as well, to ask them for *their* opinions. If they trust you to listen, young people can fully explain how they feel. With their viewpoint uncluttered by adult preconceptions, prejudices and social conventions, they can give a highly original view of the situation. They also benefit from being brought in on even the most unpleasant duties of a family, such as sick or deathbed visiting or attending funerals. They may react in embarrassing ways, sloping off in a pet or scowling the whole time, but such a response often arises only from their difficulty in coping. They haven't had your practice over the years in hiding their feelings. They may be hurting a lot *more* than you, or than you realise, at the death of a special friend. Or, they may be unable and unwilling to hide, under-neath the veneer of good manners, that they actually did dislike the person intensely. However they act at the time, being involved in an unhappy event paves the way for their being able to put it behind them.

Asking young people for their opinion, for example on the decision to move house, or on whether grandma should come to stay with you, is not the same as abdicating your responsibility to them. You have a right to your own life, and their dislike of, for instance, an intended spouse should not necessarily put a barrier in the way of a marriage. But, if you have listened to their feelings, you have far more to go on in sorting out a compromise. And inviting them to the negotiating table sets the scene for bargaining and an eventual constructive outcome. If you have explained to them how you feel, they are far more able to see your decision as a sensible and understandable one, rather than interpreting it purely as selfishness or an attack on them. And if you have heard what they have to say, you may find that they see drawbacks that you have not suspected, or for which you hadn't allowed.

Arguments are sidestepped if you listen without having to be shouted at. Whatever the crisis, you could defuse the situation by sitting down with a pre-arranged agreement. Once you have explained *what* is going to happen, *why* it is going to happen, and how you feel about this, everyone will have a chance to say how they react, and why. You may then find that not only do you get the result you want more efficiently, but that everyone is happier and more co-operative about the situation.

Very few families see their young people grow to adulthood without all of you coming under some strain or other. However, even the most extreme of crises can be weathered if you have managed to give your youngsters two gifts. The first is the knowledge that you love and value them. Emotional security will keep them afloat even when everything else seems to be falling apart. The second is skill in communication. With this, you and they will know what is going on and understand each other's viewpoints, feelings and behaviour.

8
PAYING THE PIPER
AND SHARING THE LOAD

Learning about money
and household chores

'You can't win with kids. If I don't have his best shirt washed and ironed whenever he wants it, there's hell to pay, but does he ever thank me? Does he heck! He treats this house like a hotel and me like a servant and all he ever seems to want is more money for yet another record or piece of clothing. Honestly, sometimes it makes me wonder why you have children – it's just too much hard work to be worth it.'

Jane C.

Money probably causes more arguments within families than any other subject. Husbands and wives quarrel over bills, and parents and children knock heads endlessly over even the smallest sums. Money is more than just pounds, shillings and pence and a convenient way of allowing us to convert hours of labour into food, drink and shelter. Money is power. In this society, the more you have, the greater your status.

The parent with the purse strings is the person in the household who has the final say on who does what and goes where. As long as you can promise to give, or threaten to withhold, your cash, you have control over a large part of your young person's life. This is particularly true as your children enter their teenage years and commercial pressure makes the trappings of adolescence – the clothes, the gadgets, the social life – so important.

Most families will give their young children a certain amount of pocket money each week. The amount tends to vary according to your own budget and whether or not you expect a child to save. Some parents just offer enough for sweets and comics, and buy everything else the child needs. Some give more, and insist that an amount is put away for birthdays and Christmas presents. Pocket money tends to be 'no strings attached' money – an unconsidered and automatic amount that the child can use on treats. Any other purchase must be filtered through the parent who has the control of what the child ends up owning.

In essence, the child has no personal property, it all 'belongs' to his or her parents, and is theirs to give or withhold. Money, therefore, bestows enormous control in that it allows you to maintain a hold, not only on behaviour but on taste. As the young person advances into adolescence, wresting this control from you becomes more and more important. Parents often despair at what appears to be the growing greediness of their teenagers, who seem forever to be demanding more goods. In fact, what is being demanded is buying power – the *symbol* of the money, not the money itself or the things it purchases.

As parents, we often feel that we have excellent reasons for keeping control of our youngsters' spending. After all, we say, look at that expensive jacket that was only worn once or twice! If we hand over the reins, they will only make a hash of it. This is a bit like throwing a child who has never seen water into the deep end of a swimming pool and crowing 'There you are. I said she'd never learn to swim!' as she goes under for the fourth time.

Handling money is something you have to learn slowly and carefully, under proper supervision – but that you *have* to learn to do for yourself. If you keep it a comparative mystery, you can hardly be surprised if the first time a young person has to organise their own money – in their first job or away at college – they get into a dreadful mess. Going straight from pocket money to wage or grant is a recipe for financial disaster. Most parents would like to help their teenagers learn the invaluable skills of money control by giving them a transitional experience between the two. This is best accomplished by agreeing an allowance between you, and initially supervising how they administer it.

You can usually divide the way you and your teenagers use money into three different levels. The bottom level is on trivial treats – sweets and snacks, light reading and toys. The top level is expensive items and absolute necessities – essential clothing, housing, food and transport. The middle level covers all the things you would *like* to have, and might need, but that can be subject to personal taste and the money available – various items of clothing, entertainment and some eating.

Obviously, pocket money is supposed to cover the least important items, and a wage or salary has to account for the top level. Most of the arguments between parent and child occur over middle level items, and they are the objects that could be bought by an allowance. The amount you give, and the responsibilities that go with it, can vary and increase as your youngster gets older. The principle, however, should apply from the moment pocket money stops and an allowance begins. That is, that financial freedom carries with it financial duties. Having an allowance is a way of learning how to manage money, both now and in the future.

How should you and your teenager work out a fair allowance? Comparisons with friends might be difficult, especially if some have parents who are far better or worse off than you. Probably the most effective way is for you to use your own spending as a guide. You, your partner and your teenager should set a period during which you all keep a strict record of every amount of money that is spent on that member of the family – on clothes, entertainments, hobbies and essential equipment for school or sports. At the end of a fair time – say, at least two months – you should all get together to list the amounts and the areas of expenditure. Divide these into obvious categories. For instance: *Entertainment*, such as entrance fees for discos or cinemas, videos, books, records or tapes, and some sports; *Eating*, such as snacks outside the home and some school meals; *Essential clothes*, such as school uniform, top coats and shoes and certain items such as sanitary protection; *Non-essential clothes*, such as the latest fashions; *Interests*, such as some sports and hobbies; *School equipment*, and some books; and *Miscellaneous*, such as birthday and Christmas presents, holiday money, etc.

The next stage is to decide which of these items will become the responsibility of the young person. It might be reasonable, for instance, to leave sanitary protection and some school equipment on the household budget if these are already being bought for several members of the family. Top of the list for handing over would be non-essential clothes and entertainment. As we have already seen in previous chapters, these are the areas that cause most friction, because it is your offspring's ability to make such choices of their own that becomes so important at this stage. However much you feel that they may waste their money or go against your tastes, it is in this area that you should force yourself to let go. Part of their wastrel behaviour comes from a lack of responsibility. As long as they are convinced that you can and will cough up when asked, they will continue to throw aside objects with which they are bored, and demand more. They may even do this deliberately, using your money as a weapon against you, just as you might be using it as a means of controlling them. If they have a set sum with which to replace such items, they will soon learn to pace their spending more sensibly.

You should obviously assess the amount you spend and the areas your teenagers will take on board representatively. Some months, such as over the summer holidays, or Christmas, are more expensive than others, and this should be built into a set monthly sum. Having negotiated a system, both you and your teenager have to agree on an introductory period. Both sides need to give assurances. Yours should be to sit back and resist the temptation to interfere. Unless specifically asked, you should bite your tongue and keep silent until you come back to the table for a review – in, say, three months. In return, they must agree to keep a written record of their transactions, and not to ask for more money. Three months will give your teenager a chance to make some mistakes and learn from them. It will give you all a chance to see if the amount agreed upon was fair or whether it should be adjusted, and it will give both sides an opportunity to see the advantages of this system.

For the young person, the advantages are obvious. He or she will be free to decide their own priorities and make their own choices. Instead of having to justify their tastes to you, they will have to think in terms of good value and forward planning. These are far more valuable lessons to learn than how to win an argument or wear down an aged parent! The advantages to you may be far less obvious but even more momentous. Handing over control of money removes the reason for so many arguments and disagreements. It may also save you the need to bail your youngster out of trouble in the future. And above all, it can lift a burden from your shoulders, if you are prepared to explain and share the way the family budget works.

A frequent complaint by parents is that children seem to think that money grows on trees. How else, when parents so often do not explain where their money comes from, what is needed to earn it and how much is available? The only time many children come into contact with these concepts is when the family is in real crisis, and even then they are sometimes shielded from the real implications. Young people leave lights on, doors open and indulge in ruinously long 'phone conversations because they genuinely can't grasp the fact that you have to *pay* for this. So much of their comfort is paid for by 'invisible' money that has no relation to the small change in their pockets. And your purse or pocket always seems to be full, no matter what you say in denial.

Parents would like to give their children security and confidence in them as providers and protectors. We feel hesitant at giving them a proper run-down on the family finances, partly because we may not wish to confuse them; partly because we don't want to alarm them; and mostly because we don't want them to see us as fallible! We don't like them thinking that money grows on trees when they are in a demanding mood, but we love their thinking us fully capable of giving them the best. You may feel that explaining the details of how much money you have coming into the household exchequer and what bills and commitments have to be paid out of this sum may tarnish your image in their eyes, but it will make them understand why you cannot or will not fork out the sort of pocket money they would like. In my experience, young people have far more respect for you if they can see how adults juggle their financial demands, than if they remain in ignorance.

If you want them to be sensible and thrifty, the best way is to include them. *Show* them the bills when they arrive. Obviously, you have to walk a fine line. No young person should be made to feel a burden or get the idea that their parents think of them as an expensive luxury they would be better off without. But every young person deserves to learn how a home is run. Being shown that heat, light, food, clean clothes and toilet necessities have to be bought and are not left by the elves are invaluable lessons for their future.

The allowance you assess will reflect the amount you can afford to spend on your teenager. If they want more, it is entirely reasonable that you require that they go outside the family and earn it. Some parents are willing to offer an extra amount if jobs are undertaken around the home, but you might like to consider your attitudes to this. On the one hand is the argument that, as members of a family, they have a certain share in the duties as well as the privileges. Mum doesn't get payment for the cooking of meals, nor Dad for mowing the lawn, so why should anyone else? The argument against that might be that she chose to have a family, and he chose to have a garden, neither of which applies to the youngster! The problem with giving money for household chores is that it implies that contributing towards the family's well-being is only a responsibility for some of its members. In effect, it says that parents are there to give and young people only to receive – an attitude that makes for selfishness and laziness.

At what point do you draw the line and say 'From here on, you have a responsibility'? It could also give some young people the idea that, for instance, only women should be doing housework and only men go out to work – a division of labour that most people today find unworkable. Equipping young people to pull their weight both in and outside the home should start long before they leave it. However, many parents would still prefer to give extra money in this way, rather than have their teenager go into paid employment while still in their care. In some cases, the argument is that 'childhood' is a time of innocence, free from responsibility, and it would be a pity to expose them to the hardships of commercial reality too soon. Against that is the view that young people need and want such experience, and that too often it is not the young person's innocence that is being protected but the parents' power and possession of them. They will come up against the real world soon enough. Surely it is better to do so in small doses from a safe base early on, rather than in a single, uncontrolled and unprepared-for rush when they leave school or home?

Young people can legally work from the age of 13, with certain provisos, and most will be happy to have a Saturday or morning job if it means that they have money of their own. It hardly needs to be stressed that money earned by the sweat of their own brow is *theirs* and not subject to anyone else's direction. However, in a family with genuine financial problems, most children would be proud to see their own earnings as a part of the family's income, and to relieve you of the need to give them an allowance. You would want to be assured that their job does not interfere with their education or their necessary social life, but beyond that, you should leave them to handle it their own way.

The only time you might be needed is if the job puts them at risk of any kind of exploitation. A young person in an early job may be eager to prove themself and loath to come to you for help, especially if they think you might say 'I told you so!' Some unscrupulous employers are well aware of this and might offer poor wages or conditions, or even demand harder and heavier work than the law allows, secure in the knowledge that few youngsters will complain. Worst of all, some will sexually harass their employees, knowing they will be too scared to tell their parents. The more supportive and positive you are about your teenagers taking this first step into the world, and the more you encourage them to discuss it with you, the less likely this is to happen.

If they haven't already got one, being given an allowance or taking a job are ideal times for your young people to open a bank or savings account. Banking their money not only imposes a further discipline on dealing with their finances, it also establishes them in the credit world – a very necessary step if they are to want a mortgage in the future or need banking references. If they can get an easy familiarity with the mysteries of cheque books, cards and statements at this time, they are far less likely to be frightened or overawed later in their lives. They can also have the opportunity of meeting and getting to know their bank manager before the jokes and remarks of colleagues at work paint this creature as a terrifying ogre to be avoided.

If learning to manage a budget is a preparation for the future, so too is learning how to run a home. But just as letting go of control over money can be painful, so sharing household chores can also cause anxiety. Mothers particularly can see the running of a home as their own special preserve, and take a possessive pride in being a good wife and mother.

Many of the disagreements between mother and teenager are due, not because he or she is unusually messy or inconsiderate, but because Mum refuses to adjust to a new pattern. If you are angry because a meal is wasted or because a room is untidy, who is at fault? Your teenager, for wanting to go out on a Saturday night and to keep his or her room in the state that suits them? Or you, for persisting in making a hot meal on an evening you should have realised was committed to outside pursuits, and in continuing to see your role as housekeeper as essential? Mothers can have endless arguments with their teenagers about the tidiness of rooms and the cleanliness of clothes. This can become impossible, with you at permanent screaming pitch about the mess, and them in a permanent sulk at your 'nagging.'

There is one easy way to stop the argument, but it does

require that you change how you see your role as Mother. What you need to do is to abdicate responsibility for their territory. Their room is to become their preserve, and its tidiness or cleanliness is their business. As long as this does not spill over into the rest of the house, you will leave them to get on with it. Of course, if clothes are not excavated from the heap and brought to

you, they cannot be washed. If the bed is not stripped, they will sleep on dirty sheets. If cups and glasses disappear into the black hole, they must drink straight from the tap. Sooner or later, your teenagers will begin to see the personal benefits of a certain amount of order. They will never do so, however, as long as you continue to do the work for them.

There are two ways of keeping your youngsters dependent on you. The obvious first way is by maintaining a grip on their money. The second is by keeping them incapable of looking after themselves – of denying them the ability to wash, cook and clean for themselves. There is immense satisfaction in being the one to deliver the freshly ironed shirt to the newly cleaned room, and in dishing up the favourite meal – and equal pain when inevitably the young person starts rebelling and rejecting these offerings.

Many parents complain of being taken for granted and used like servants and hotels, not recognising that it is their own actions that have set up this apparent selfishness. If you insist on being the only ones to do this work around the home, how can you expect your youngsters to see it as anything other than your job and their right? If the sharing of chores is not something that has happened in your home since their childhood, introducing it now might need careful discussion and preparation. But if you want to ready your teens for a happy future, you owe it to them to start soon. There are better reasons to set up home with a partner than just because *he* needs someone to cook the meals and she needs someone to change plugs and fix the car!

Handing over responsibility for money and asking your young people to bear some weight for running your home is a form of rite of passage. By doing this, you recognise that they are capable of being included in some important aspects of adult life and are a valued and valuable part of the family. By trusting them in this most potent of areas, you make them feel able to come to you with confidences in this and other 'adult' matters.

9
ROMANTIC PLACES
AND FAR AWAY PEOPLE

Family holidays
versus solo adventures

'I wasn't looking forward to our holidays this year, but they turned out to be the best ever. For a start, me and the wife went off on our own for a week, and then we met up with the boys in a village in France – they'd been hitching around with some friends for a few weeks beforehand. We hadn't been keen on their going off on their own, but there they were, safe and sound, having had a whale of a time. I don't think we stopped chattering the entire fortnight, and we didn't have a single argument, and I can't remember ever being able to say that before.'

Phillip N.

Up until their teenage years, children tend to accept fatalistically that holidays are something that adults plan and visit upon you. For many, family holidays are a special treat, as they are often the only time they get to spend an extended period in both parents' company. Holidays are usually equally important to you, in offering the opportunity to enjoy your family without the interruptions of work or school, and the strains that these can impose on you all. In the absence of stressful routine, families are often able to relax and appreciate each other as they cannot do for the rest of the year.

However, as adolescence progresses, young people begin to realise that leisure time off school, college or work is something *they* can anticipate and organise for themselves. Their increasing explorations in friendships and pursuits mean that they want or need to spend time with people other than their families. Young people live on a very short time scale. To you, an interruption of a few weeks during summer may be trivial – you can return to take up any loose ends in your social life and resume as before. A teenager may well find a particular person or group has moved on beyond their reach, or a special and important event has taken place without them, and find this devastating. It is no use your saying that if a friendship is that fragile it isn't worthwhile – to a young person; 'length of service' is not the standard by which they measure. A friend or interest can be vitally important *at the time*, even if your teenager then goes on to lose interest after a few months.

For this reason, teenagers may suddenly become argumentative about your holiday plans, and sullen and sulky during the time you are away. If they do ask permission to go on a separate holiday with friends or to bring a friend along, you may be tempted to refuse, insisting that the family stays together. Carrying an unhappy teenager under duress on holiday is like having a parcel full of rotten fish – not ignored easily, and difficult to transform into pleasant company. So, now may be the time to examine your attitudes to family holidays, holidays themselves and the basis of any fears you might have about your sons or daughters going their separate ways.

Our insistence on sticking together can often, and dangerously, be due to an idealised image of the joys of the family holiday. We are very good at editing our memories, keeping the beautiful, peaceful and enjoyable recollections and conveniently forgetting the arguments, the moments of boredom and the frustrations. We recall holidays with our own parents, and with our children when younger, in this distorted fashion. They may well have been glorious, but repeating an earlier experience can often fail, particularly when the participants and the surroundings have developed and moved on. Even if your early memories *were* accurate, you could be in for a disappointment if you insist on attempting to recreate them. If they were not, you might be in for a disaster. Different times form different tastes, and your teenager may well have developed specific interests at an earlier age than you did, and want to use their leisure time to explore these.

If you do want to offer them a family holiday that would appeal, you might find that this is the time to break from the past, as a way of formally acknowledging they have grown older and your relationship with them has changed. Instead of just being a time to *be* together, your three or four weeks of holiday can become a time to talk and to experience something new and exciting with your emerging adult offspring. The first step in achieving this is to invite their ideas on what they would like to do and where they would like to go.

Choice of holiday can often provoke a power struggle, open or hidden, that echoes in the family for the rest of the year. Some people prefer a rest – two or three weeks on a beach, soaking up the rays and doing nothing more strenuous that eating, drinking and turning brown. Others would like to explore the country-side, take up a new skill or practise a sport. We tend to be fairly conservative about what we do in our leisure time, and many people cling to the belief that a rest means being inactive. This can be particularly frustrating for the teenager who is going through a period in life when their mind and body needs constant stimulation. Parents could learn from their young people the unobvious truth that running about, getting physically exhausted and filling up your mind with new impressions is ultimately far more relaxing than lying about doing nothing.

Rather than just inviting the youngsters in your family to have a say in the refinements of destination – that is, between one Mediterranean village and another – why not invite their ideas on the *type* of holiday you take, and the part of the world it should be in? It may also be worthwhile to discuss length of holiday. Both you and your children might find the limits of tolerance at this time are stretched less by two short and different holidays in a year, than by one long marathon. Negotiation and compromise can play a part here, with you agreeing to go on the holiday of their choice if they submit to yours.

Giving your young people a say in the type and location of your holiday can make agreement easier for all of you. So, too, can inviting their active participation in the running of the holiday itself. If everyone is to enjoy themselves, a useful

strategy is to give each person the right to choose and plan at least one day's activities. The responsibility – and power! – can be exhilarating in itself, and the opportunity to introduce the rest of the family to a particular pastime can be fun. If such a plan is agreed beforehand, you also have less risk of enduring the sulks and tantrums of 'But we always do what *you* want'.

It can also be productive to let your teenagers go off on their own, exploring or making new friends, or even to stay behind at the hotel or beach while you go on excursions or spend time with people your own age that you have befriended. Being with your offspring on holiday can be enormously enjoyable, but spending time alone with your partner has a special flavour of its own. You may well benefit from making the effort to give yourself time away from the kids to cherish each other's adult company.

The entry of your young people into adolescence is the first stage on a journey they make to leave you. Rather than having to do it all at once, it could be valuable for you to begin to revive the pleasures and skills of being alone together, over this period. It can still be a family holiday if you only meet up to be together over meals, or on selected evenings, afternoons or mornings. Part of the excitement would then lie in reporting and sharing each others' separate discoveries, and in giving advice and suggestions on what to do next. If you adopted this scheme, allowing your teenager to bring a special friend with them would thus add to everyone's enjoyment. Rather than their being seen as an interloper who breaks up the happy unit, they introduce a new viewpoint and provide safe company for your son or daughter.

Having some say in where you holiday together, and having some control over part of your time together may not be enough. The chances are that at some point your teenagers will bring up the subject of going their own way. Your objections may have a reasonable basis. You might fear that they could not cope on their own, whether the suggested excursion is a package tour abroad or a week spent camping or youth hostelling in Britain. Specific anxieties can range from their losing their money, losing their way to losing their virginity. Objections, however, can also spring from the somewhat ignoble emotions of jealousy.

Young people still in full-time education have more leisure time than adults at work – around 12 to 20 weeks a year as opposed to your 3 to 5 weeks. It isn't difficult for you to feel that their having the extra treat of a holiday on top or instead of the family get-together would be spoiling them. They see it as an essential way of making use of or passing the long free period.

Young people today have far greater opportunities for travel and exploration than we did. There are fewer social restrictions on mixed or unmarried groups of youngsters staying together, and the range of places and activities that are accessible and affordable has increased, making the opportunities of our own youth look positively underprivileged in comparison. It may not be anxiety for their well-being that makes you uneasy at letting them go, but envy. If you feel that the extra holiday away from you is spoiling them, consider this. You may resent their wanting more than you have already spent on the family holiday, but however much you have laid out, did *they* consider it money well spent, or was the only person truly satisfied, yourself? If money is the problem, there is nothing wrong in insisting that they take a job during some of their holiday periods or on weekends during the year, to save up for their own adventures.

If you are worried about their ability to cope, the best way of dealing with this is to train them to take such responsibility. You don't save your children from drowning by forbidding them to go near water – you teach them to swim and to understand basic water safety rules. If they ask to be allowed to go on holiday with friends, the most effective strategy is to give provisional permission on the understanding that they must come up with proof that they can plan, organise and control their time away from you. They need to be able to show they know where they are going, with whom and what they will be doing. They need to demonstrate that they have a grasp of their financial and health needs, and can sort out any disagreements or problems that can come up.

If you agree to negotiate, and accept that they are old enough to take responsibility for themselves to a certain extent, they in turn should agree to a series of sensible checks and controls on your part. You may ask them to make regular 'check-in' 'phone calls or to report in to a neutral adult on the spot, for instance. If the young person is going to be moving from place to place, it's quite reasonable for you to request a copy of the proposed route and for them to inform you if there is any deviation – a sensible precaution if, say, illness in the family means they have to be contacted.

Having agreed in principle, arrange an initial planning session with the young person and their friends and, if possible, the other parents involved. At this they should lay out their ideas and answer any questions you might have. They may be full of unformed enthusiasm, but have a limited grasp of the essentials at this stage. Instead of putting them down or withdrawing your permission, give them confidence and solid advice and send them away to perfect their ideas.

As in most dealings with teenagers, there is a fine line to walk between helping them to make their own decisions, and taking over the project yourself. How they handle the preparations for a holiday or expedition is a good guide to how they will manage the event itself. In the last analysis you can always use your veto and postpone it until later if you don't feel they are aware of all the ramifications. They are more likely to accept such a decision if you have given them some leeway. They can see your point, and learn from their mistakes, only if you let them see for themselves how ill-equipped they are, and how experienced they will have to become to cope on their own. School excursions are often an ideal practice for holidays with friends. They give young people the 'half-way house' experience of being organised and looked after in their practical needs and in having much of their time dictated, but also in being left to themselves to sort out some of their activities and in having to get along with their peer group. However expensive they may seem, they are often good value for teaching these vital lessons.

The unvoiced fear behind much of the resistance to teenagers going off on their own on holiday is that they might exploit this licence and become sexually active. As the flood of letters that hits the desks of agony aunts every September can testify, the holiday romance is indeed a serious danger. A group of young people going away together can often egg each other on with exaggerated tales of sexual adventures, and elaborate plans for future conquests. The tragedy is that much of this is empty boasting, and it is often those with the least experience and the least ability to cope with the consequences who seek to impress their friends by actually going ahead.

Holiday romances, however, are not just the result of showing off. Being on holiday has a distinct effect on our romantic tendencies, whether we are 16 or 60. It can remove our inhibitions, and the freedom from stress and routine, the influence of beautiful surroundings and exotic food and drink all relax us. Most people take particular care of their appearance on holiday and are very conscious of their own and other people's bodies. In putting on special clothing, we put on a new image and a new persona. Somehow, what we do while away can be left behind when we go home, especially since it is unobserved by our local gossips! We may feel able to act in ways that we would never entertain back home.

People of both sexes can find themselves becoming more emotionally involved and physically freer with a new acquaintance at short notice, than they would in their own familiar surroundings. Being on holiday gives you the opportunity to live out your fantasies and to claim you are older, wealthier, more experienced and better employed than in reality. Fears of pregnancy, of what the neighbours or your family will say, or of catching a sexually transmitted disease, do not intrude on such a fantasy.

There are two important points to note. Firstly, none of this can be confined to holidays *away* from parents. The effect can be simmering beneath your very nose in your own hotel, and the only way you could guard against it would be to watch over your teenager's every move. This would blight your holiday as well as theirs! Secondly, it isn't only teenagers who fall for this trap. Adults do too, if they have never had the chance to consider what they are doing. You may protect your offspring throughout their teenage years by overseeing their holidays, only to have them severely hurt on the first holiday they take away from you as a grown up. If you want to protect them now and in the future, the best way is not by mounting guard, but by bringing the subject out into the open and discussing it with them. Young people are likely to be more wary and choosey if they are aware of the insidious effects of sun, sea and palm trees – or sun, snow and ski poles – on their emotions. Life guards, waiters and ski instructors always seem attractive, and can have new bed partners every week of the season from those taken in by their fractured English, practised charm and air of sophistication. A broken heart can possibly be avoided if you could help both your sons or daughters to separate the possibility of a real 'love at first sight' from just the heightened sensations of an exciting holiday.

Warning young people not to drive fast does not always stop them from being involved in a car crash. However, advocating the use of a seat belt could forestall their needing plastic surgery or losing their lives. Similarly, the worthy advice and moral homily might not prevent them from allowing themselves to be carried away. If you feel that discussing practical precautions would only encourage them to go too far, or that the consequences of unprotected sexual intercourse are a fit punishment for that crime, then you may well have to endure your offspring suffering an unintended pregnancy or a sexually transmitted disease. They, of course, will suffer far more than you for your moral stance. In my experience, discussing contraceptive precautions with young people and offering them supplies, actually *prevents* more sexual activity than it ever encourages, because it drives home the significance of their behaviour. When young people have to consider the results of an action, they often consider the action itself far more thoughtfully. On the whole, young people want commitment in their relationships, and can only be taken in if they have not been given the opportunity to think about and discuss what it will mean. Carrying a packet of condoms is not a badge of promiscuity, nor a prompt to activity – but it could be the one barrier between them and HIV, the virus that can cause AIDS, or parenthood.

Planning for their own holidays is yet one more part of the apprenticeship for adulthood. Encourage them to spread their wings in this way, and you are more likely to find that in a few years' time *they* are insisting you all take a family holiday together 'just like we used to do'. The best way to ensure your family fight to have your company is to allow them to avoid it sometimes!

10
QUALIFIED SUCCESS

The modern dilemma of education and employment

'We're at loggerheads at the moment because he wants to leave school and join this firm that a friend's father has started up and we're insisting that he stays and gets his exams. He'll thank us in the end, because there's no substitute for proper qualifications.'

Ronald S.

Your offspring, by law, are entitled to full-time education up to the age of 19 and, until they are 16, this is *your* responsibility. We want the best for our children, but we and they may not always agree on what this is, and what is the best way to achieve it. We may not even be clear, ourselves, on what they need to be successful in adulthood. Certainly we expect that their years in school will equip them to get on in the outside world, and we usually demand that they have some sort of qualification to show at the end of their education. But what do we mean by 'qualifications', and how best can we help them to gain what is necessary?

When we talk about qualifications, most people think in terms of certificates showing exam successes. It is still true that certain jobs and opportunities are accepted to be only open to those with a certain number of recognised examination passes. However, even entrance to university is more flexible than most people realise. A mature student with no examination passes at all could be taken on if he or she could prove application, enthusiasm and basic understanding and knowledge. More important, the job market has changed drastically in the last ten or 20 years, and new skills are becoming more valued than many 'proved' by conventional examination results. Young people can find themselves in an unpleasant quandary in that lack of qualification can deny them a job, but having such a certificate no longer *guarantees* them one. So, your offspring may have a real point if they argue that passing their exams is a waste of time.

It is no longer true that high earning and high status are only accessible to those who undergo long training and gain high qualifications. Nor, it must be added, that high earnings are any longer a proof of merit! In our day, there was still a fairly recognisable distinction between manual and 'white collar' employment. A desk job had more status and was expected to carry greater rewards, if not in immediate money, then at least in security and eventual increments. The division between the machine and the pen has been blurred by the rapid spread of technology. It is now possible for a young person leaving school at 16 with nothing to show but natural ability, to take advantage of on-the-job training and end up better equipped, of higher status, with a far greater salary and brighter prospects, than someone who has gone the full route of further education. In fact, in areas such as computing, academic teaching is not always able to keep pace with developments in the field. Some graduates entering this profession may find themselves more at a disadvantage than a less 'qualified' colleague with practical experience.

One reaction against our age of mass production has been the increased demand for handmade goods or personalised services. Young people with a practical skill or an entrepreneurial turn of mind can find themselves in a sellers' market, and are more likely to be admired and fêted for their talents than looked down on for using their hands or living off their wits.

As parents, we have come from an age group that has known extended, if not full, employment. A job, or the reasonable prospect of one, was a normal expectation. We subscribe to what is often called The Protestant Work Ethic – we believe that people *should* work for their living or to keep their families. We also feel that our identity is defined in terms of our employment. That is, you are not so much John Smith, father of two and husband of one, but John Smith, doctor or machine fitter. People without a job, in this view, are without an acceptable identity. They are either layabouts, scoundrels or failures.

Our very first question on meeting a new person is still often 'What do you do?', and by that we mean what is your *paid* occupation. People whose daily efforts are not rewarded with a paypacket or salary cheque are often extremely apologetic, whatever their reason for being in that situation. Even though she is engaged in one of the most difficult and worthwhile jobs of all, a woman bringing up a family is liable to belittle herself by saying 'Oh, I'm only a housewife.'

The labour market has changed considerably, however, since we were young. Technological advances have meant that we need a smaller workforce to run our society and to produce even more goods than the larger one used to do. The pool of people needed to run our society will get smaller still – but we continue to judge people as if not having a job was a matter of choice when often, and increasingly, it may not be. The obvious solution would be to spread the burden of work more thinly over a wider number of people. Whether we take up this challenge and drastically change the nature of employment by making use of part-time or job-sharing schemes, or whether we go on as now with the 'haves' in work and the 'have nots' out of it, the fact is that a greater number of people will spend a greater amount of time out of the workplace. 'Spare' time will soon become main time, which means that we really must start training our young people to enjoy and make use of this leisure.

For a start, instead of seeing themselves as members of a profession or job, perhaps we could encourage youngsters to find a particular interest that involves them and to pursue that as their main identity. Instead of being employed or unemployed, they could be a 'badminton player' or a 'martial arts student'. Or even better, 'I'm Joe Bloggs, a very nice person to know.' Whether we are fully employed or not, we often find our greatest satisfaction in the things we do in our 'spare' time. So it is often ridiculous that we assume that this part of our lives is incidental or of less real importance than our paid employment. When it means that people having difficulty in finding employment, or who are surplus to the labour requirements at any one time, suffer enormously from the feeling that they are at fault or inferior, this attitude is possibly harmful, not only to individuals, but to society as a whole.

Young people are often aware of these dilemmas and will argue that there is no point in pursuing qualifications 'because it's a waste of time, and who wants a boring job anyway?' Be honest, how many of us really do enjoy our work? How much of our anger at 'social security scroungers' is based on the understandable irritation at their apparently having a life of ease while we labour away at jobs we don't enjoy but feel we ought to do? Might it not be better if some of us took the opportunity to spend more time improving ourselves and doing things we always wanted to do, and part in giving our time to help others in volunteer, charity work or community schemes? You remain in the boring job to get money to buy possessions – some of which you may not even want. Your offspring may be willing to pay the price of having fewer things, in order to buy other than material satisfaction. This does not make him or her less ethical than you. It just means they have a different moral viewpoint.

Part of this could be the recognition of the importance of skills not directly related to work. One of the most important jobs any adult can undertake is also the one for which we are often the least prepared – being a parent. It is assumed that parenting 'comes naturally', which is a ridiculous underestimation of an extremely skilled 'profession'. If we spent less time worrying about fitting our youngsters for the labour market, maybe we could devote more attention to helping them gain the far more valuable skills of communicating, getting on with other people and being able to bring up their own children.

In spite of the fact that their 11 to 13 years of school education is supposed to equip them to cope with an independent existence, school life often holds them back from being able to do so. Pupils are often still treated as children – beings too young to be trusted with any responsibility more onerous than keeping track of their own pencils. At the time when we say we expect them to be involved in decisions and choices that could affect the rest of their lives, we actually demand obedience, discipline and acceptance.

School children are thought to be without knowledge, and their task is to accept the bounty knowledgeable adults offer them. There are exceptions, but in the main young people are not asked to express any ideas of their own, for it is felt that the relatively uninformed nature of their opinions makes them valueless. This means that many young people never have the chance to *develop* the skills involved in making decisions and gathering facts to form a reasoned opinion. The transition from school to further education or employment, where they *will* be asked to organise their own time, take responsibility and generate their own work, may then be a shock. Many are left floundering, without the necessary skills or even the awareness that such are needed. Education is all too often a question of accepting facts without expecting an explanation, rather than a training in how to gather, interpret, and use facts yourself.

The sad aspect of much of traditional schooling is that, by making discipline and authority the most important element, you actually incite and invite pupils to rebel. If you succeed in keeping them under control, it is often not order you achieve, but mindless passivity. Adolescence being a time of questioning, you either have to work very hard to keep such enquiry in bounds, or work equally hard responding to it. When adolescents are given free rein, they can turn on, and want to examine, many of our most cherished institutions – such as marriage, religion, family life or work. This is why we often feel anxious or uneasy at allowing them to step over strict boundaries. Teachers and parents who do so, often find the experience exhilarating and revitalising, and that they learn as much as they teach. Far from being negative or destructive, such examination can give you a fresh viewpoint or allow you to reaffirm or adjust your values, without just taking them for granted.

Many teachers are trying new approaches in attempts to make education a true learning experience rather than just a question of 'I say. You listen.' We may find the idea of less formal lessons, or even teachers being addressed by their first names, gimmicky or ineffective, but with adolescents, such an approach is often more productive than stricter lines.

Young people also often find it easier to adjust to the different demands of approaching adulthood if they are in a school where a sharp distinction is drawn between the rest of the school and the fifth and sixth forms, or where they can do their final years in a sixth-form college. When the school keeps pace with the degree of responsibility or the social behaviour of its older students *outside* school, a better relationship between pupil and teacher can be achieved. When he or she is being given a certain measure of responsibility and respect, and allowed privileges in the form of relaxation of rules and uniform, the student is more likely to see the task of learning as something that benefits them and can be enjoyed, rather than a boring irrelevance. All too often, teachers and pupils find themselves cast as opponents wanting to outwit each other, rather than partners with a common aim.

Some parents may pay lip service to the goal of 'getting on', but consciously or unconsciously sabotage their offsprings' educational career. You may openly encourage them to do their homework, but find yourself in a perplexing and losing battle, and finally take the soft option and leave them alone. The problem is that young people admire and copy their parents and are inclined to do what you *do*, not what you *say*. Parents who hardly ever read a book, rarely do paperwork, are faintly contemptuous of 'serious' programmes on television and denigrate 'boffins' or 'clever dicks', give a message *against* education which no amount of encouragement to do homework will overcome.

Even the most bookish of families can hold back their youngsters if they continue to demand that their young people aspire to qualifications that might be irrelevant to what the teenager wants to do in life.

For this reason, it really is important that you listen to your young people and appreciate their own ambitions and needs. It

can be very easy to visit upon them our own ambitions, either in genuine wishes for their own good, or as thinly disguised devices to fulfil our own frustrated aims. Alternatively, it can be equally beguiling to allow jealousy of their opportunities to show in snide comments and a refusal to allow them to make full use of what is being offered by the school.

It can be particularly baffling to find your son or daughter set on a vocation that in our day was only open to members of the other sex, and to feel that this is either a slight on their masculinity of femininity, or a mistake. You do need to free yourself from recourse to the cry 'In my day . . .'. The world our teens are facing has little or no resemblance to the one we encountered in our adolescence, and places very different demands. To gain their ear and their respect, it is often necessary for you to be able to admit your ignorance and ask for *their* help in understanding their problems. Reading their magazines and books can give you an insight into the influences and interests that motivate them. Talking to their teachers can give you the information you need to help your offspring with their decisions, and discussion with a professional careers guidance officer can often give valuable ammunition.

When a young person leaves school, they have some 40 to 50 years of potential working life in front of them. This is ample time for them to make at least a couple of career moves, several 'first millions' and half a dozen early retirements. There is *always* a second chance. If they can enter this major part of their life with enthusiasm, self-confidence and the ability to think for themselves, they may be better equipped than if they had one specialist qualification, and no 'oomph'.

Although you have every right to closely question a young person who wants to give up a particular course of study, you should be open to their reasons. They may seem to you to be trivial – a dislike of a certain teacher, or a sudden nervousness because none of their friends will be in the same class. They may seem quite alarming – an outbreak of bullying in or outside the school that makes your teenager's attendance unpleasant or even dangerous. They may also be excellent – a *genuine* feeling that a particular teacher or course is inadequate, or a change of direction (little Jane or Johnny may not *want* to be a doctor any more!).

Courses in the sixth form or at college could also be a revelation. There are thousands of jobs or professions that we hardly know exist, and new ones are being created every day by new technology and the expanding service industry. All these are areas that you and your teenager should try to discuss, over which you should negotiate to reach a solution that satisfies you both.

In the case of a disagreement with a teacher, you could help your young person to resolve this by role playing the best way to handle it. If this fails, you could act as a go-between to reach some sort of understanding. Dealing with bullies may respond to the same strategies, although in some cases you might have to ask the school or the local police to become involved.

If your teenager is dissatisfied, try not to dismiss their opinions or feelings out of hand. You may be right in thinking that what they need is a bit of persistence and application. Their best interests may lie in sticking it out, and a few well chosen words on the fact that life *can* be hard work, may at times be boring and that we all have to do things we don't always relish, could do the trick! They are more likely to listen to what you have to say, however, if it comes out as part of a discussion rather than a one-sided lecture. Asking them to put their point of view can be illuminating to both parties. If their unhappiness does not have a sound basis, they themselves are likely to work this out and realise that continuing the course they are on may be the best option. If they cannot explain their reasons, but feel they are right, you can ask them to think it over and come back. If they do have reasons that make sense to themselves, you may well find that some sort of compromise is in order – a new course, a new class or a new college. If they have already started to absent themselves from school or college and play truant, it is all the more important to try to sympathise with and understand them, however much you might disagree with their actions or reasons.

For many of us, security is all. We aspire to a safe job and a pension, and the knowledge that this will always be there. For many young people, security can be sacrificed for a greater flexibility and interest. The greatest qualification we can offer our teenagers is to help them to be 'do-ers' – active people willing to take a chance and become involved – not 'wait-ers' who hang around expecting 'them' to shape and manage their lives.

11
LEAVING HOME

The first steps
to total independence

'I dreaded their going. I didn't know what I was going to do with my time and I knew the place would seem so empty. But then I got a job that I really enjoyed and Steve and I found we had so much more money between us and time to spend, that it was like starting life all over again. I love it when they come home, but I'm happy that they are enjoying their lives too.'

Liz B.

As the end of adolescence approaches, most young people will consider the prospect of leaving home. Some will long for the freedom a place of their own seems to offer, and some will shy away from the responsibilities and hard work they realise is entailed.

It could be argued that you can measure the success of parenting a child by the amount of care, guidance and protection that has been given, but the success of parenting a teenager by the degree with which you have gradually stepped back and let them go it alone. The way they take to looking after themselves, and their ability to cope, and how you face up to the fact of their leaving could be seen as your Graduation Test.

Your young person is likely to have to leave at some point – to go to college, to seek work or to form a family of their own. Even if none of this applies, most emerging adults do feel the need to establish their own base as a final step in the journey from childhood to adulthood. Whether they launch off sooner or later, with your consent or in the wake of arguments, with success of failure, is largely in your hands. It is your attitude to their leaving, and the efforts you have made to teach them how to look after themselves and a home that may dictate all this.

Some parents make such a comfortable home for their late teenagers that they find it extremely difficult to think of leaving. Such a parent is always on hand with a duster, clean clothing and a hot meal, and is ever-ready to slip junior a few pounds. Such a parent congratulates themself on being so good at their job of providing a loving, comfortable home that their children never want to leave them. To be needed is seen as the greatest compliment.

The problem is that only dependent children need their parents in this way. While catering to a child when it is not capable of looking after itself is admirable, refusing to develop a young person's ability to look after itself, to artificially prolong such dependency, is not. When a young person coddled in this way *does* eventually venture forth, he or she can find living in the real world confusing and even painful, and may feel little gratitude for your silken cords. Young people of both sexes who have been over-protected are quite likely to find themselves in poor relationships and marriages. They will be seeking another Mother or Father to do everything for them as their parents have done, rather than looking for an equal mate with whom they can share their lives. They may also charge into an ill-advised marriage, seeing it as the only way they will be able to break free of you.

Being needed by your children may be satisfying when they are young, but a far more rewarding feeling when they are older is the knowledge that your efforts have made it possible for them to do without you. Young people who cannot cope on their own are likely to feel resentment and bitterness mixed in with the love they have for their parents, and to struggle to get away. Young people who have been given the confidence and the opportunities to step out alone in life are likely to return regularly, out of choice rather than need, and show their respect and gratitude as well as their unforced love.

If your teenagers show no signs of flying the nest, you may have to give them a hearty push. There is nothing cruel or unnatural in insisting that it is time that they start looking after themselves. If both of you find it hard, it may be necessary for you to look honestly at what is going on. If they are clinging or taking advantage, it can only be with your encouragement or connivance. It's no good complaining of their presence if you also continue to cater to their needs. Some parents find it helpful to 'give notice' to their offspring – 'find your own place by such and such a date or you're out on the street!' – to give both sides a chance to prepare for the big step.

There are two levels of preparation for your young person's leaving – the emotional and the practical. And both of these must take place in you and them. They need to know that one day soon you are expecting them to make a life of their own, and to be offered insights into how much organisation and money this can require. Clean clothes and hot meals, toothpaste and soap, heating and lighting, do not appear spontaneously. They must be planned for, shopped for and paid for. Young people can be cavalier about all such items, wasting them and grumbling if they are not there, because often they just do not realise what is involved in making everyday comforts available. The first few months in a place of their own can be a nightmare, as they constantly reach for items they have always taken for granted, only to find them missing, and the necessary money and time already frittered away on entertainment or clothes. This is why it really is necessary to involve both young men and women from their earliest years in the running of a home, to show them the household bills and to explain to them the use of household money.

Your teenager also needs to see that *you* are anticipating their move, and see it in a positive light for yourself. Obviously, they would be hurt if you made them feel that you were only waiting to see the back of them to start enjoying life to the full. But equally it can be a frightful burden for a teenager to have the impression that their parents' entire existence revolves around them. Some parents do see their children as an insurance policy, guaranteeing them love, company and status. They neglect friends and a social life of their own, to heap all their hopes on their offspring. In such a case, the young person is terrified to go, emotionally blackmailed into believing they would be the cause of their parents' loneliness and lack of purpose. So, not only do you need to accept that it is part of the natural order of things that your children leave you, but you should make your own preparations for the time when you will again be a two or one-person household. Rather than relying on them to bring in company, new ideas and entertainment, you and your friends should make your own.

The practical preparations for a young person leaving home will also be another test of your ability to walk that fine line between offering essential advice, and in taking over what should be your young person's experience. As with many other aspects of growing up, they need to make some mistakes for themselves and to feel that they are in charge of their own actions. You are a resource to be called upon when they need you. Pushing yourself too far forward could well provoke an apparently disproportionate response. As with so many parent/ teenager arguments, their anger would be at your questioning their ability to cope for themselves, rather than at the particular incident itself.

Finding a place of their own can be tedious and complicated. Working through the red tape of college applications, or searching through newspapers and noticeboards for rented property and then choosing the new home, can be difficult. Dealing with inventories, deposits and terms of lease with a landlord so much older than themselves can often be overawing, but if you do it for them you set a pattern that may prove counter-productive. Your guidance and advice, and perhaps your presence as a witness and safeguard, are preferable to your taking the leading role.

You are riding shotgun, not driving this particular waggon!

Since looking for accommodation is such a complicated area and there are so many different avenues to explore – council housing, private renting, renting through an agency, housing co-operatives, council and private mortgages and even legal and illegal squatting – you need to do some research yourself to feel confident to offer up-to-date and realistic advice. The picture may be very different, depending on the part of the country in which you live, and whether the youngster wants to stay in the country or a town. So, local knowledge is essential. You can get the best advice from the nearest Council Housing Department, Citizens Advice Bureau, Law Centre, Student Union or Young Men's or Young Women's Christian Association (YMCA or YWCA).

Once your teenagers have flown the nest, it can be very tempting to paper over any shortcomings in their ability to care for themselves by continuing to do so yourself. The son who brings home his washing every weekend, the daughter who calls round several nights a week to enjoy a hot meal and a warm bath, are so commonplace that advertisers use these images to sell rail cards and stock cubes! But is this a tribute to your warm and wonderful personality, or your willingness to be a perpetual servant? And what does it say about their attitudes towards themselves and you? Obviously, young people need a gradual introduction to the rigours of adult life, but this is best achieved while they are still at home, rather than left until the last moment.

A particular sore point with many young people is the degree to which their parents consider their new home an extension of parental property. Many parents are used to feeling that they have the right to move freely about their young person's room, since it is they who pay the rent or mortgage. Parents who have contributed to the new home, by finding it, paying for it or furnishing it, are particularly prone to assuming they should be able to walk in at any time, and alter anything as they choose. This is not helpfulness or generosity – it is an intrusion, and is likely to be met with simmering resentment or outright fury. It is particularly objectionable if it demeans the young person's ability to cope in the eyes of their flatmates or friends. The young person will probably delight in asking you to visit. They may be grateful for suggestions or practical help, but the key is to make it clear that this is available, and then wait for it to be requested, rather than pressing it upon them uninvited.

Your children will always be in a special category, but in many ways imagining the sort of good manners you would extend to and expect from an unrelated guest or friend can give you a guideline as to how to behave in order not to offend them. You wouldn't expect even a best friend to allow you to turn up unannounced, to rearrange the furniture and criticise the scones. Offer the same courtesy to your own offspring. As a way of underlining their new status, you might ask for the same good manners back. Without putting any barriers in the way of your young people coming to visit you, or asking for help when they definitely need it, it would make them feel less like rats leaving a sinking ship if they could see that you, too, have an active life and sometimes need notice before they call round.

As long as they stay under your roof, your offspring will conduct their relationships under your rules – or at least be seen to do so. Although the vast majority of young people acquire and choose to live by their parents' moral or social code, details such as when to get up in the morning, when to retire at night and what constitutes an enjoyable get-together with friends can differ. Once they have their own living accommodation, they may well embark on a routine you could find bemusing. Most young people are carried away by the novelty of organising their own lives. Rather than your rushing to judgement and interfering, they are more likely to settle down and apply a reasonable discipline if left to find out for themselves that study or work and late nights don't mix.

A more contentious and less easily resolved difference of opinion may well arise over their romantic relationships. In reality, we and our teenagers are closer in behaviour than you might think. Two studies published in the late seventies showed that although 33 per cent of parents of teenagers disapproved of premarital sex, and 56 per cent had mixed feelings, almost three quarters of couples married in the early seventies – the parents of today's teenagers – had sex with their husbands before the wedding. We are often happy to condemn an action we have enjoyed ourselves and that did us no harm, merely because, as in the story of the emperor's clothes, nobody is prepared to go against the crowd and say 'But, I disagree with that!' Teenagers today, however, not only largely agree with sex before marriage, they are more prepared to be honest and open about it than members of our generation. How are you to act when introduced to a girlfriend or boyfriend who is obviously having a sexual relationship with your adolescent, and with whom they may even be living?

Some parents take the unbending path. They make it clear that any evidence of such a relationship would be most unwelcome, and cue their offspring to deceive them. The partner is sent packing when Mum and Dad pay a visit, or has to pretend to be just another friend. Other parents do bend, but into the ostrich position. No comment is made if it is clear that the two young people are sharing a bed on their own territory, but on visits to the parental home, separate sleeping quarters are *de rigueur*. This usually results in another level of deceit, with one of the young people involved tip-toeing through the house in the dead of night and just before dawn, to snatch a brief moment of intimacy. Some parents trust in their upbringing of their offspring, and accept that if he or she is having a sexual relationship, it must be of some value, and allow the couple to share a room in their house.

Such liberalism can be misinterpreted, but allowing your young people to carry on in the open as they do amongst themselves is *not* the same as encouraging or inciting licence or unruly behaviour. On the contrary, it removes the need for deceit and encourages them to behave in as honest and considered a manner as possible. Forcing them into holes and corners promotes hole-in-the-corner sex, and it is denying the reality of what we do in private that leads to hyprocrisy and intolerance. You may find treating them in an open way is difficult and embarrassing, and your first encounters with their partner could well be strained. This may be even more true if your offspring's lover turns out to be of the same sex or a different race – two areas that strike at many of our unconscious prejudices. The choice you may have to make is which is more precious to you – your youngster and your relationship with them, or your moral code? To a degree, you can ask any guest entering your door to conform to the house rules, but there comes a point in your dealings with your offspring when insisting they hold to your values means insulting theirs and denying their separate identity as caring, intelligent human beings.

Of course, there may be circumstances which make it impossible for your teenagers to leave your home, even when they have effectively left your control in other ways by getting a job, going on to higher education or even getting married. A shortage of money or available accommodation could mean that they must still share your home. In such a case, you might find the tension between you increasing unless you mutually acknowledge that a new stage in their life has been entered, and adjustments should be made. It might be useful for all parties concerned to sit round a table and thrash out some new agreements on how you will live together. Because the domestic routine seems to go on as before, it can be hard to see the need for any adjustments. They are necessary, however. Either because without them you may find arguments increasing, as your offspring long for self-determination in their daily life and kick against your routine. Or, because if they do *not* complain, it is likely to be because you are 'institutionalising' them – that is, accustoming them to being looked after by other people.

To avoid either of these ultimately unpleasant and destructive options, you and they might come to a series of agreements over a new way of dovetailing your lives. In return for being allowed to set their own schedule of comings and goings, your offspring might take the responsibility for getting some of their own meals, doing their own cleaning and washing and contributing realistically towards household expenses. They and you might also experience greater enjoyment if, once in a while, they undertake to plan, buy, cook and serve a family meal. You might find it an aid to your memory that times have changed if this new allocation of responsibility went hand in hand with a new division of territory.

If it is at all possible, giving the maturing teen a room away from the rest of the family could emphasise the fact that they need and deserve privacy to carry on their own life. You might also help them to re-equip what was once just a bedroom, to make a bed-sit where they can invite their friends. In even the smallest house and the least well-off family, such things can be improvised. The important key is to recognise that the person responsible for the behaviour and well-being of the young person concerned is now themselves, rather than you. If both you and the young person can make this conceptual jump, matters such as saying when one or other will or will not be in for a meal or will be late home become areas of common courtesy rather than a struggle for control or meat for an argument.

There is a saying that children are not our property but are only lent to us for a time. If we have been 'good enough' parents and discharged our duties as their trustees, we will be happy to finally hand over the reins, secure in the knowledge that they can cope, to their true owners – themselves.

A FINAL WORD

This book may seem to concentrate on the problems, arguments and frustrations of being the parent of teenagers. After all, who turns to a book for information or advice when they don't anticipate, or aren't experiencing, difficulties? However, this is *not* to say that being a parent of an adolescent is necessarily a constant battle. On the contrary, it can be the best part of being a Mum or Dad and make the hard work and the sacrifices most parents willingly make for their family thoroughly worthwhile. But, forewarned is forearmed. Seeing what you have thought to be inexplicable or inevitable arguments explained in somebody else's words, can often help even the best families get along just a little bit better.

We often view adolescence as being a phase that has to be got through on the hurried journey from childhood to adulthood. This is a pity, since the sense of urgency and impermanence turns this age into an impediment or embarrassment to be put behind you as quickly as possible. It may only last for a few years and be a time of enormous change and upheaval. None the less, adolescence is a state to be savoured and enjoyed, by both teenagers and parents. Participants and onlookers would be so much happier if we could iron out the difficulties before they happen and so encourage each other to enjoy the results.

Adolescence is a time that should be taken seriously. Many of the attitudes formed now will persist for the rest of their lives. Central and fundamental feelings – how they see themselves, how they view and treat others and whether they find sexual relationships and friendships pleasurable or traumatic – will all have their foundations in these years. If you can instil in your young people a respect for themselves and a respect for others, by giving them *your* respect . . . you will have earned the title A Good Enough Parent!

GLOSSARY OF SEXUAL TERMS

bag	scrotum
balls	testicles
being careful	withdrawal or coitus interruptus
blow job	oral sex (woman to man or man to man), fellatio
bollocks	testicles
bonking	having sexual intercourse
bringing yourself off	masturbation
bumming or buggery	anal intercourse
clap	gonorrhoea, but often used to describe any form of sexually transmitted disease (STD)
climax	having an orgasm
clit	clitoris
cobblers	testicles
cock	penis
cock cheese	smegma, a discharge around the penis
come	semen; or to have an orgasm
coming	having an orgasm
condom	contraceptive sheath
crack	vulva
cunt	external female sexual organs, vulva
dick	penis
dose	STD
Durex	contraceptive sheath
dyke	female homosexual, lesbian
fag, faggot or fairy	male homosexual
fanny	vulva
fiddling	masturbation
finger fucking	mutual masturbation, or manually stimulating a woman
French kiss	deep kissing
frigging	masturbation by, or manual stimulation of, a woman
fuck	sexual intercourse
gay	homosexual (male or female)

159

hand job	manually stimulating a man
hard on	erection
head (usually, give head)	fellate, oral sex usually woman to man or man to man
horn (have the)	erection
horny	to be sexually excited
jack off	masturbate
jam butties	period
jerk off	masturbate
jism	semen
johnny or jolly bag	contraceptive sheath
knob	penis, specifically the glans
knockers	breasts
lay	to have intercourse; one's sexual partner
lezzie	female homosexual, lesbian
noddy	contraceptive sheath
nuts	testicles
on the rag	having a period
pansy	male homosexual
pills or pillocks	testicles
poof, poofter or pouf	male homosexual
prick	penis
pubes or pussy	vulva
queen or queer	male homosexual
rag	sanitary towel
screw or shag	have sexual intercourse
shooting your load	to ejaculate
sixty-nine	mutual oral sex
slag	derogatory term for a woman
slit	vulva
slut	derogatory term for a woman
spunk	semen
stones	testicles
straight	heterosexual
stud	laudatory term for a man
tits	breasts
tool	penis
tossing off	masturbation
twat	vulva
wank	masturbate
willy	penis

SUGGESTIONS FOR FURTHER READING

For you:
Families and How to Survive Them, Robin Skynner & John Cleese, Penguin
Teenage Pregnancy in Industrialised Countries, a study sponsored by the Alan
   Guttmacher Institute, Elise F. Jones & others, Yale Press
Teenage Pregnancy in Britain, Judith Bury, Birth Control Trust
Games People Play, Eric Berne, Penguin
The Art of Starvation, Sheila Macleod, Virago
How to Get Off Drugs, Ira Mothner & Alan Weitz, Penguin
Living with Grief, Dr Tony Lake, Sheldon Press
The Relate Guide to Second Families, Suzie Hayman, Vermilion
Stranger in the Family, Terry Sanderson, The Other Way Press

For you and your teenager:
Growing Up, Dr James Docherty, Modus Books
Why Suffer: Periods and Other Problems, Lynda Birke & Katy Gardner,
   Virago
Acne, Paul van Riel, Sheldon Press
So You Think You Are Attracted to Your Own Sex?, John Hart, Penguin

For your teenager:
Making It: How to Handle Love, Tricia Kremman, Pan
Teenage Body Book, McCoy & Wibblesman, Piatkus

For your teenagers' teachers:
Taught Not Caught – Strategies for Sex Education, The Clarity Collective,
   Learning Development Aids
Sex Education – Some Guidelines for Teachers, Dilys Went, Bell & Hyman

SOME USEFUL ADDRESSES

There are plenty of professional and self-help groups, ready and willing to help and advise both you and your teenager – together or separately – on any aspect of their development. Some are national groups, and many have London addresses. This *doesn't* mean that there is no help in your area if you live elsewhere. Contact the main address and they will be able to put you in touch with your *nearest* help.

You can look in your local 'phone directory for the following:

Social Work Departments

If you have any family problem and would like to talk to a local social worker or counsellor, look under the name of your own Council, or under 'Social Services Departments'.

Sexually Transmitted Disease or 'Special' Clinics

These are usually found under 'VD' or under the local hospitals listing.

Community Health Council

If you want any help with your or your teenager's health, or advice in dealing with the family doctor or any health problem, look under 'CHC' or the name of your local Council.

Samaritans

If you are at your wits' end, find the Samaritans' number in the 'phone book, or just ask the operator to put you through. And if you fear your teenager is coming to the end of their tether, leave the number in view.

Help with the Physical and Sexual Changes of Adolescence

Health Education Authority,
Hamilton House,
Mabledon Place,
London WC1H 9TX
Tel: 0171–383 3833
Produce many excellent pamphlets and books on healthcare and health-related problems.

Family Planning Association,
2–12 Pentonville Road,
London N1 9FP
Tel: 0171 837 5432
Helpline: 0171 837 4044
Can send books and leaflets on all aspects of sex and sexuality. They will
also have the address of your nearest birth control or youth advisory clinic.

Brook Advisory Centres,
165 Grays Inn Road,
London WC1X 8UD
Tel: 0171 833 8488
Helpline: 0171 410 0420
Offer birth control clinics especially for young people. They can also give
help with pregnancy and relationship problems.

Parents Friend,
c/o V.A. Leeds,
Stringer House,
34 Lupton Street,
Leeds LS10 2QW
Tel: 0113 267 4627
Offer help to young people or parents in coming to terms with someone in
the family being gay.

London Lesbian and Gay Switchboard,
Tel: 0171 837 7324 (24-hour service)
or write to them:
BM Switchboard, London WC1N 3XX
For someone who is gay or thinks they may be gay and needs someone to
talk to. There are now local lines in most parts of the UK.

Help with the Emotional Upheavals of Adolescence

Relate–National Marriage Guidance,
Herbert Gray College,
Little Church Street,
Rugby CV21 3AP
Tel: 01788 573241
Can offer sympathetic help for *any* relationship or sexual problem to
parents *or* young people.

Parent Network,
44–46 Caversham Road,
London NW5 2DS
Tel: 0171 485 8535
Support for parents at any stage of family life. Self-help groups and courses.

Help with Problems Due to Adolescence

Eating Disorders Association,
Sackville Place,
44 Magdalen Street,
Norwich NR3 1JU
Tel: 01603 621414
For sufferers of anorexia and bulimia nervosa and their families.

National Association of Citizens Advice Bureaux,
115–123 Pentonville Road,
London N1 9LZ
Tel: 0171 833 2181
Can help and advise on any subject. They have centres nationwide.

Children's Legal Centre,
University of Essex, Wivenhoe Park,
Colchester CO4 3SQ
Tel: 01206 873820
Offers advice and information on the law affecting children and young people.

Mind,
Granta House,
15–19 Broadway,
London E15 4BQ
Tel: 0181 5192122
Can offer advice and support on all aspects of mental illness.

Association of Community Health Councils,
30 Drayton Park,
London N5 1PB
Tel: 0171 609 8405
For advice and information on local health services.

The Patients' Association,
8 Guildford Street,
London WC1N 1DT
Tel: 0171 242 3460
Will help with problems you may have with the National Health Service.

Women's Therapy Centre,
6 Manor Gardens,
London N7 6LA
Tel: 0171 263 6200
Deals with a wide range of female problems, including eating disorders.

The National Association for Pre-Menstrual Syndrome
PO Box 72
Sevenoaks,
Kent TW13 1XQ
Tel: 01732 741709

Childline,
Tel: 0171 239 1000
Helpline: 0800 1111

NSPCC,
Child Protection Helpline,
Tel: 0800 800 500
Counselling services for incest victims and their family.

London Rape Crisis Centre,
PO Box 69,
London WC1X 9NJ
Tel: 0171 837 1600 (24 hours)
    0171 278 3956 (office hours)
A counselling service for women who have been raped or sexually abused.

The Terrence Higgins Trust,
52–54 Grays Inn Road,
LondonWC1X 8JU
Tel: 0171 242 1010 (helpline)
Counselling and information on all aspects of AIDS.

British Pregnancy Advisory Service,
Austy Manor,
Wootton Wawen,
Solihull,
West Midlands B95 6BX
Tel: 01564 793225
A private charity that will offer abortion advice if the family doctor or birth-control clinic cannot help.

One Parent Families,
255 Kentish Town Road,
London NW5 2LX
Tel: 0171 267 1361
Offer advice and support to the single parent.

Help with Family Problems

National Stepfamily Association,
Chapel House, 18 Hatton Place,
London EC1N 8RU
Tel: 0171 209 2460
        0171 209 2464 (counselling line)
Advice and support for step-parents and their children.

National Council for the Divorced and Separated,
13 High Street,
Little Shelford,
Cambs. CB2 5ES
Tel: 0116 2700595
Will help anyone involved in a divorce or separation.

Women's Aid Federation,
PO Box 391,
Bristol BS99 7WS
Tel: 0117 963 3494
Provides information, refuge and support for women who need to leave
physically or mentally threatening situation.

CRUSE – Bereavement,
Cruse House,
126 Sheen Road,
Richmond, Surrey TW9 1UR
Tel: 0181 940 4818
For sympathetic advice and help with a death.

National Society for the Prevention of Cruelty to Children,
42 Curtain Road,
London EC2A 3NH
Tel: 0171 825 2500
Local NSPCC workers will help in any case of cruelty to young people.

Help with Alcohol and Drugs

Al-Anon Family Groups,
61 Great Dover Street,
London SE1 4YF
Tel: 0171 403 0888 (24 hour)
Helps to cope with an alcoholic in the family.

Alcoholics Anonymous,
PO Box 1,
Stonebow House,
York YO1 2NJ
Tel: 01904 644026
Have local self-help support groups for the problem drinker who wants to stop.

Action on Smoking and Health (ASH),
109 Gloucester Place,
London W1H 3PH
Tel: 0171 935 3519
Will give help and advice on how to stop smoking.

Accept National Services,
724 Fulham Road,
London SW6 5SE
Tel: 0171 371 7477
Will help with advice and addresses on any drink or drug problem.

The Standing Conference on Drug Abuse (SCODA),
32–36 Loman Street,
London SE1 0EE
Tel: 0171 928 9500
The main source of up-to-date information on where to get help with drug problems.

Release,
388 Old Street,
London EC1V 9LT
Tel: 0171 729 5255
     0171 603 8654 (emergency)
Can help with drug, legal and abortion problems.

ADFAM National,
32–36 Loman Street,
London SE1 0EE
Tel: 0171 928 8900
Can help if someone in the family is a drug taker.

Families Anonymous,
The Doddington and Rollo Community Association,
Charlotte Despard Avenue,
London SW11 5JE
Tel: 0171 498 4680
Can help if someone in the family is a drug taker.

Help with Education and Careers

Advisory Centre for Education,
22–24 Highbury Grove,
London N5 2EA
Tel: 0171 354 8321
For information and advice on school or college courses.

Higher Education Information Centre,
Middlesex Polytechnic,
Queensway,
Enfield,
Middlesex
Tel: 0181 804 8131
Offers information and advice on what college courses and grants are available.

Open University,
PO Box 200,
Milton Keynes,
Bedfordshire MK7 6YZ
Tel: 01908 653231
Offers second chance to those who missed out on university to catch up by doing a degree course at home. Exam qualifications are not needed to be accepted on a course.

INDEX